AN EGYPTIAN CHILDHOOD

AN
EGYPTIAN CHILDHOOD

The Autobiography of
Taha Hussein

Translated by E. H. Paxton

HEINEMANN
LONDON
THREE CONTINENTS PRESS
WASHINGTON D.C.

Heinemann Educational Books Ltd
22 Bedford Square, London WC1B 3HH

IBADAN   NAIROBI
EDINBURGH   MELBOURNE   AUCKLAND
HONG KONG   SINGAPORE   KUALA LUMPUR   NEW DELHI
KINGSTON   PORT OF SPAIN

ISBN 0 435 90228 8 (AWS)
ISBN 0 435 99416 6 (AA)

First published in English by G. Routledge and Sons 1932
First published in Arab Authors 1981

Published in the United States of America 1981
by Three Continents Press
4201 Cathedral Avenue, N.W.,
Washington D.C.

ISBN 0–89410–211–7

British Library Cataloguing in Publication Data

Taha Hussein
    An Egyptian childhood. – (African Writers Series; 228 :
    Arab Authors; 16)
    1. Egypt – Social life and customs
    I. Title   II. Series
    962'.04'0924   DT70

ISBN 0–435–90228–8 (AWS)
ISBN 0–435–99416–6 (Arab Authors)

Set in Linotype Juliana
Printed in Great Britain by
Willmer Brothers Limited
Rock Ferry, Merseyside

Introduction

Taha Hussein was born on 14 November 1889 in Izbit il-Kīlō on the outskirts of the town of Maghāgha in Upper Egypt. He belonged to a large family of very modest means and, blinded in early childhood by the clumsy ministrations of the local barber/surgeon, he seemed destined for a limited religious education of a traditional type, and for a stunted life. But he soon broke out in a direction of his own choosing, and – as educator, reformer, thinker, and writer on many subjects – he blasted a trail that led, through many tribulations, to wide recognition as a leader of modernism and to many national and international honours.

He was, in fact, the first graduate of Egypt's first modern university, later the first Egyptian to become Dean of its Faculty of Arts, and later still the first Egyptian to be nominated for a Nobel Prize in literature. The first volume of his autobiography was the first piece of modern Arabic writing to be recognised as a masterpiece, and its English translation was the first accolade it received from outside the Arab world.

Thirty years ago, his prolific and seminal output provided me with the ideal subject – clearly definable, and at the same time substantial and central to the field – for the first doctoral dissertation in a western university and the first book in a European language[1] on any aspect of modern Arabic literature.

With the views I expressed then, Taha Hussein and his family have never been entirely pleased, although I take it as a mark of their toleration and qualified confidence that I am entrusted with the writing of this introduction. I do not myself consider the judgements I reached then as being unduly severe. The stature of a man who achieved and inspired so many 'firsts' is self-evident, but it would be anomalous if the ideas he expressed in more than sixty books and in the heat of some fierce polemics on political, educational and literary issues had always been correct or even fully thought out.

If an overall corrective is needed to my early assessment of Taha Hussein's work, it lies in the historical perspective which the lengthening years have brought. I had occasion recently to write of the generation of Arab intellectuals of which he was the most representative and most immediately influential member:

> They were not cautious philosophers or meticulous scholars, but bold spirits casting their bread upon the waters. Their greatness was in their open-mindedness, their courage, their tenacity. Their achievement was that they swept away a conservatism part of which at least badly needed to be swept away; they accustomed an entire generation to thinking along new lines.[2]

Of the qualities that enabled Taha Hussein to leave his mark on an entire nation, his sensitiveness and independence of spirit shine through every page of his autobiography. What is not immediately evident from this source alone is the magnitude of the mental obstacles he had to overstep, the dedication and toughness he needed, and the price he had to pay for fulfilling his potential.

The early articles and poems which Taha Hussein published between 1910 and 1913 while he was still a student have seldom been taken into account in overall estimates of his career. This is because he never had them reprinted in book form,[3] indeed he disowned them in later years, asserting – perhaps with undue severity – that poetry had never been natural to him[4] and that he was ashamed of the vehemence of his attacks on the leading prose-writer of the time, al-Manfaluti.[5] These early outbursts reveal him as a headstrong youth, more fiery than compassionate – so outraged, for example, at the government's decision to licence prostitution that he could invoke the full rigour of Islamic law:

> Visit its judgements upon every wrong-doer;
>   Let not half-heartedness turn you back.
> Lapidate and flog as God commands,
>   And you shall be spared whoredom and debauchery.[6]

Nevertheless, we have here a necessary starting point for measuring the immensity of the strides he was soon to take. Thus, in a series of articles published in *al-Hidaya* in 1911 on the position of women in society, he was already arguing stoutly against their veiling and for extending to them the benefit of education. Yet, while acknowledging that Islamic law had always allowed Muslim men to marry Christian or Jewish women, he was alarmed at the possible influence that European wives might have on Muslim husbands at a time when his compatriots had lost their cultural stability and self-confidence and were hell-bent on aping European ways, so that he concluded:

I have no doubt that we need to exercise extreme caution in availing ourselves of this provision—namely, that a Muslim may marry a woman who adheres to a Scriptural religion. Indeed I see no harm in asserting that it is now sinful and hateful to do so. Many of us marry European women of Scriptural faith because we desire them for their beauty, their reputed intellectual and cultural attainments, and the like. But what is the result of such a marriage? Nothing but the transformation of the man together with his household, his sons and his daughters, into Europeans through and through – except in the case of a handful of unusual individuals, too few to take into consideration in formulating general rules.

I can therefore proscribe marriages of Muslim men to European women of Scriptural faith or at least severely restrict their incidence, especially if to what I have said is added that faith has become so thoroughly corrupt in Europeans as to be almost non-existent.[7]

Less than seven years later, he had himself married a French-woman who has remained a devout Catholic, yet to whose beneficial influence he has repeatedly paid tribute,[8] and he was launched on a vigorous career in the course of which – by dint of challenge, exhortation and example – he provided Arab Modernism with its most appealing formulation: not Innovation but Renovation, the revitalisation of a great cultural heritage by bringing the best modes of Western thinking to bear upon it, and this in emulation of forefathers who, in the heyday of Islam, had drawn freely on the resources of Greek civilisation.

Sustaining him through this tempestuous career was the belief – perhaps naive but firmly held, and shared by many of his contemporaries – in the duty and the power of the intellectual to reshape his society by fearless assertion of the truth as he sees it. From this ideal of service Taha Hussein never departed, and from its cost he never flinched. Thus, during a particularly difficult period stretching from March 1932 to November 1934, when the government of the day not only deprived him of State employment but also tried to inhibit his lecturing and journalistic activities, his friend, the French Orientalist Louis Massignon wrote to him raising the possibility of an academic position in the United States; Taha Hussein considered this for three days then decided against it, explaining to his wife: 'In America, I would be a foreigner, a spectator of the country's life, not a participant in it; I would have only a limited duty to perform.'[9]

The same dutifulness informs many of his writings. It was as a conscious attempt to fill a gap, to test Arabic as a vehicle for new literary genres, that he published a volume of epigrams,[10] even though his style was not best suited to terse expression. I once surmised that it was similarly because he was not cut out to be a playwright that he devoted so many of his efforts as a critic and translator to the service of the theatre. His family confirms that he did at one time plan to write a play in collaboration with Tawfiq al-Hakim, but what they produced instead was a fanciful book-length narrative toying with the Sheherezad theme.[11]

His autobiography might also have been specifically designed to enrich the Arab literary tradition, for the genre was virtually unknown in it.[12] In reality, however, it derives from a set of circumstances which illuminate another aspect of Taha Hussein's character.

He initiated so many controversies and pursued them with such zest and vigour that it is easy to overlook how much they cost him both materially and emotionally. He revealed in 1966[13] that the first volume was dictated while holidaying in France but harassed by reports of the campaign mounted against him in the Egyptian press and Parliament by men who considered his earlier book on pre-Islamic poetry to be impious. It seems that he buried himself in the task as if to escape from his worries, completing it in nine days. I have it from his family that he then showed the manuscript to his friend Abd al-Hamid al-Abbadi, who advised against its publication, presumably because of the very humble background it revealed. The reticence, I believe, was the expression not of snobbery but of a deeply ingrained traditional Islamic view that poverty may be no disgrace, but advertising it is. We have reason to be grateful, nevertheless, that Taha Hussein disregarded his friend's counsel. From the time it was first published – serially in al-Hilal, between December 1926 and July 1927 – it encountered enormous and well-deserved success.

A second volume followed soon after;[14] it was also dictated when Taha Hussein was out of sympathy with the government in power. Other autobiographical material is scattered in the casual articles he used to write while holidaying in Europe. A notable example is the description of an incident in which a small group of young Azhar students, fresh from the provinces and full of zeal for the faith, set out for the prostitutes' quarters one evening to preach repentance, only to flee in panic when the women, highly amused, advanced upon them with taunts and mocking invitations.[15] The treatment is full of verve and humour, in startling contrast to the youthful poem I quoted earlier.

A third volume, entitled *Memoirs* and first printed in Beirut in 1967, was Taha Hussein's last book-length publication.[16]

Taha Hussein died on 28 October 1973, only days before his 84th birthday, an age which he had hoped to reach in order to match the record of the eleventh-century poet al-Ma'arrī who, like him, had been blind and with whom he had long felt a special kinship.[17] Although highly honoured by President Abd el-Nasser, he had held no political office since he was Minister of Education in 1951-2. Especially as editor-in-chief of the daily *al-Jumhuriyya* until 1964, he did have his say on the problems that exercised the minds of intellectuals after the 1952 Revolution, and to the very end he presided with devotion and distinction over the deliberations of the Arabic Language Academy. But – beset by ill-health and, after a spinal operation in 1961, very much restricted in his movements – he had, in the last fifteen years of his life, written no major study and initiated no great controversy. Nevertheless his funeral cortege was followed by thousands who – for all that he had long been out of the limelight – sensed that his name was inseparable from the new momentum acquired by Arab self-awareness in modern times.

PIERRE CACHIA
Professor of Arabic Language and Literature
Columbia University, New York

NOTES

1 *Ṭāhā Ḥusayn: His Place in the Egyptian Literary Renaissance* (London, Luzac, 1956).

2 'The assumptions and aspirations of Egyptian Modernists', in *Islam: Past Influence and Present Challenge*, ed. A. T. Welch and P. Cachia. (Edinburgh, Edinburgh University Press, 1979), p. 223.

3 Others, however, have made efforts to collect them and comment on them; see notes 6 and 7 below.

4 Interview reported in *aṭ-Ṭalaba l-'Arab*, 5 March 1966.

5 In a radio interview in 1949.

6 Quoted in 'Abd al-Mun'im al-Qabbānī, *Ṭāhā Ḥusayn fī ḍ-ḍuḥā min shabābih* (Cairo, al-Hay'a l-Miṣriyya l-'āmma li l-kitāb, 1976), p. 155.

7 Quoted in Muḥammad Sayyid Kīlānī, *Ṭāhā Ḥusayn ash-shā'ir al-kātib* (Cairo, Dār al-qawmiyya l-'Arabiyya, 1963), p. 153.

8 She has recently returned the compliment in a volume of emotional reminiscences entitled *Avec toi*, translated into Arabic by Badr ad-dīn 'Arūdakī, revised by Maḥmūd Amīn al-'Ālim, and published as *Ma'ak* (Cairo, Ma'ārif, 1979).

9 Suzanne Taha-Hussein, *Ma'ak*, p. 101.

10 *Jannat ash-Shawk* (The Garden of Thorns) (Cairo, 1945), p. 26.

11 *Al-Qaṣr al-Mashūr* (The Enchanted Castle) (Cairo, Dār an-nashr al-ḥadīth, 1937).

12 A notable exception is the twelfth-century *Kitāb al-I'tibār* by Usāma b. Munqidh, translated by Philip K. Hitti as *An Arab-Syrian Gentleman and Warrior in the Period of the Crusades* (New York, Columbia University Press, 1927), and re-issued as *Memoirs of an Arab-Syrian Gentleman or an Arab Knight in the Crusades* (Beirut, Khayat, 1964).

13 Interview reported in *at-Talaba l-'Arab*, 5 March 1966.

14 Translated by Hilary Wayment as *The Stream of Days* (London, Longman, 1948).

15 *Fī ṣ-Ṣayf* (In summer) (Cairo, Hilāl, 1933), pp. 49–52.

16 It has been translated by Kenneth Cragg as *A Passage to France* (Leiden, Brill, 1976).

17 See p. 9.

One

He cannot remember the name of the day nor is he able to place it in the month and year wherein God placed it. In fact he cannot even remember what time of the day it was exactly and can only give it approximately.

To the best of his belief, the time of day was either dawn or dusk. That is due to the fact that he remembers feeling a slightly cold breeze on his face, which the heat of the sun had not destroyed.

And that is likely because notwithstanding his ignorance as to whether it was light or dark, he just remembers on leaving the house, meeting with soft, gentle, delicate light as though darkness covered some of its edges.

Then that is also likely because he just seems to remember that when he met with this breeze and light he did not feel around him any great movement of people stirring, but he only felt the movement of people waking up from sleep or settling down to it.

However, if there has remained to him any clear distinct memory of this time about which there is no cause to doubt, it is the memory of a fence which stood in front of him and was made of maize stems and which was only a few paces away from the door of the house.

He remembers the fence as though he saw it only yesterday. He remembers that the stalks of which this fence was composed were taller than he was, and it was difficult for him to get to the other side of it.

He also recalls that the stalks of this fence were close together, as it were stuck together, so that he could not squeeze between them. He recollects too that the stalks of this fence stretched from his left to an ending he could not conjecture; and it stretched from his right to the end of the world in that direction. And the end of the world in this direction was near, for it reached as far as the canal, which fact he discovered when he got a little older. Now this played a great part in his life; or shall we say in his imagination?

All this he remembers, and he remembers how envious he was of the rabbits which used to go out of the house, just as he did, but were able to traverse the fence by leaping over it or by squeezing between the stalks to where they could nibble what was behind it in the way of greenstuffs, of which he remembers particularly the cabbage.

Then he remembers how he used to like to go out of the house at sunset when people were having their evening meal, and used to lean against the maize fence pondering deep in thought, until he was recalled to his surroundings by the voice of a poet who was sitting at some distance to his left, with his audience round him. Then the poet would begin to recite in a wonderfully sweet tone the doings of Abu Zaid, Khalifa and Diab, and his hearers would remain silent except when ecstasy enlivened them or desire startled them. Then they would demand a repetition and argue and dispute. And so the poet would be silent until they ceased their clamour after a period which might be short or long. Then he would continue his sweet recitation in a monotone.

He remembers too that whenever he went out at night to his place by the fence, there was always bitter grief in his soul because he knew only too well that his entertainment would be curtailed as soon as his sister called him to come indoors. He would refuse, and then she would come out and seize him by his clothes while he resisted with all his might. Then she would carry him in her arms as though he were a plaything and run with him to the place where she put him down to sleep on the ground, placing his head on the thigh of his mother, who turned her attention to his poor weak eyes, opening them one by one and pouring into them a liquid which hurt him but did no good at all. But although he felt the pain he did not complain or cry because he did not want to be a whimperer and a whiner like his little sister. Then he was carried to a corner of a small room and, his sister having laid him down to sleep on a mat on which had been spread an eiderdown, put another coverlet on top of him, and left him inwardly bemoaning his fate. Then he began to strain his hearing to its utmost, hoping that he might catch through the wall the sound of the sweet songs which the poet was reciting in the open air under the sky. Eventually sleep overcame him and he knew no more until he woke up when everybody was sleeping, his brothers and sisters stretched about him snoring loudly and deeply. He would throw the coverlet from his face in fear and hesitation because he hated to sleep with his face uncovered. For he knew full well if he uncovered his face in the course of the night or exposed any of the extremities of his body, they would be at the mercy of one of the numerous evil sprites which inhabited every part of the house, filling every nook and cranny, and which used to descend under the earth as soon as ever the sun began to shine and folk began to stir; but when the sun sank to his lair and people retired to their resting-places, when lamps were extinguished and voices hushed, then these evil sprites would come up from under the earth and fill the air with hustle and bustle, whispering and shrieking. Often he would awake and listen to the answering crows of the cocks and the cackling of the hens and would try hard to distinguish between these various sounds, because sometimes it was really the cocks crowing, but at others it was the voices of the evil sprites assuming their shapes in order to deceive people and tease them. However he did not worry his head about these sounds or bother about them, because they came to him from afar, but what really did make him afraid were other sounds which he could only distinguish with the greatest effort, sounds which proceeded softly from the corners of the room. Some of them were like the hissing of a kettle boiling on the fire, others resembled the movement of light articles being moved from place to place, and again others sounded like the breaking of wood or the cracking of stems.

But his greatest terror of all was of persons who, in his imagination, stood in the doorway of the room and blocked it and began to make various noises something like the performances of dervishes at their religious exercises. Now he firmly believed that he had no protection from all these terrifying apparitions and horrible noises unless he wrapped himself up inside the coverlet from head to toe, without leaving any hole or crack between himself and the outer air, for he did not doubt but that if he left an aperture in the coverlet, the hand of an evil sprite would be stretched through it to his body and catch hold of him or poke him mischievously.

And so on account of these things he used to spend his nights in fear and trepidation unless he fell asleep; but he did not sleep very much. He used to wake up very early in the morning, or at any rate as soon as dawn broke, and he used to spend a great part of the night between these terrors and his fear of the evil sprites until at last he heard the voices of the women as they returned to their houses after filling their water jars at the canal, singing as they went 'Allah ya lail Allah' (My God! What a night! My God!). By this he knew that dawn had begun to peep and that the evil sprites had descended to their subterranean abodes. Then he himself was transformed into a sprite and began to talk to himself in a loud tone and to sing as much of the song of the poet (as he could remember) and to nudge his brothers and sisters who were lying around him until he had woken them up one by one. And when he had accomplished that, there was such a shouting and singing and hustle and bustle, a veritable babel, that was only restrained when the sheikh,[1] their father, got up from his bed and called for a jug of water in order to wash himself before praying.

Then only were voices hushed and the movement quietened down until the sheikh had completed his religious ablutions, said his prayers, read a portion of the Quran, drunk his coffee and gone to his work. But as soon as ever the door closed behind him the whole family rose from their beds and ran through the house shouting and playing, scarcely distinguishable from the feathered and four-legged inhabitants of the house.

Two

He was convinced that the world ended to the right of him with the canal, which was only a few paces away from where he stood ... and why not? For he could not appreciate the width of this canal, nor could he reckon that this expanse was so narrow that any active youth could jump from one bank to the other. Nor could he imagine that there was human, animal and vegetable life on the other side of the canal just as much as there was on his side; nor could he calculate that a grown man could wade across this canal in flood without the water reaching up to his armpits; nor did he conjecture that from time to time there was no water in it. Then it would become a long ditch in which boys played and searched in the soft mud for such little fishes as had been left behind, and so had died when the water had been cut off.

None of these things did he ponder, and he was absolutely certain in his mind that this canal was another world quite independent of that in which he lived. A world that was inhabited by various strange beings without number, among which were crocodiles which swallowed people in one mouthful, and also enchanted folk who lived under the water all the bright day and during the dark night. Only at dawn and dusk did they come up to the surface for a breath of air, and at that time they were a great danger to children and a seduction to men and women.

And among these strange creatures also were the long and broad fish which would no sooner get hold of a child than they would swallow him up; and in the stomachs of which some children might be fortunate enough to get hold of the signet-ring that would bring them to kingship. Now hardly had a man twisted this ring round his finger before two servants of the genie appeared in the twinkling of an eye to carry out his every wish. This was the very ring which Solomon wore and so subjected to his will genies, winds and every natural force he wished.

Now he liked nothing better than to go down to the edge of this canal in the hope that one of these fish would swallow him and so enable him to get possession of this ring in its stomach, for he had great need of it. ... Was he not ambitious at least to be carried across the canal by one of the genie's servants in order to see the wonders on the other side? On the other hand he shrank from the terrors he must undergo before he reached this blessed fish.

However, he was not able to explore along the bank of the canal for a great distance, inasmuch as both to right and to left the way

5

was fraught with danger. For to his right lay the Aduites, people from Upper Egypt who lived in a big house and had two large dogs which were always on guard at the door of the house, barking incessantly. They were a by-word among the neighbours for ferocity, for a passer-by had only escaped from them with much difficulty and hardship.

And to the left were the tents of Said-al-Araby, about whose evil doings and cunning there was much gossip, as also about his blood-thirstiness. His wife, Kawabis, wore a great nose-ring and used to frequent the house and kiss our friend from time to time, causing him much pain and no small dismay by her nose-ring. And although he had the greatest dread of going to the right and encountering the two dogs of the Aduites, or of going to the left and encountering the evil of Said and his wife, Kawabis, still he used to find in every part of this somewhat limited and restricted world of his, various kinds of amusement and games, which would occupy the entire day.

The memory of children is indeed a strange thing, or shall we say that the memory of man plays strange tricks when he tries to recall the events of his childhood; for it depicts some incidents as clearly as though they had only happened a short time before, whereas it blots out others as though they had never passed within his ken.

For example, our friend remembers the fence and the cultivated land which lay alongside it and the canal which marked the end of the earth, and Said, and Kawabis and the Aduite dogs; but when he tries to recollect the passing of all these things he cannot grasp anything. It is just as though he went to sleep one night and woke up to find no sign of the fence or the field or Said or Kawabis. And lo ! he saw in place of the fence and the field houses and well-ordered streets, all of which were on a slope stretching from north to south down to the embankment of the canal for a short distance. He remembers many of those who used to live in these houses, both men and women, and even the children who used to play in these streets.

Moreover, he remembers that he was able to explore boldly in both directions along the bank of the canal, without fear of the dogs of the Aduites or the cunning of Said and his wife; and he remembers how he used to spend many pleasant and happy hours every day on the canal bank listening to the songs of Hassan the Poet, who used to sing all about Abu Zaid, Khalifa and Diab while he was raising the water by means of a shaduf to irrigate his lands on the opposite bank. How more than once he was enabled to cross this canal on the shoulder of one of his brothers without recourse to the 'ring of kingship', and more than once he went to a place on the opposite side where stood some mulberry trees, of the delicious fruit of which he ate. How he more than once went along the bank of the canal to the right as far as the schoolmaster's orchard and not infrequently ate some apples there, and used to gather mint and basil, but he is totally at a loss to remember how this state of affairs changed and how the face of the earth was altered from its former appearance to this present one.

Three

He was the seventh of the thirteen children of his father, and the fifth out of the eleven children of his father's second wife. He used to feel that among this enormous number of youths and infants he had a special place distinct from his brothers and sisters. Did this position please him or did it annoy him? The truth is that he cannot definitely say, nor is he now able to form a correct judgement about it.

He experienced much tenderness and consideration from his mother, and from his father lenience and kindness, and his brothers he felt were somewhat reserved in their conversation and dealings with him. But he found side by side with this tenderness and consideration on the part of his mother a certain amount of negligence sometimes, and at others even harshness. And side by side with the lenience of his father he found a certain amount of negligence also, and even severity from time to time. Moreover, the reserve of his brothers and sisters pained him because he found therein a sympathy tainted with revulsion.

However, it was not long before he learnt the reason of all this, for he perceived that other people had an advantage over him and that his brothers and sisters were able to do things that he could not do and to tackle things that he could not. He felt that his mother permitted his brothers and sisters to do things that were forbidden to him. This aroused, at first, a feeling of resentment, but ere long this feeling of resentment turned to a silent, but heartfelt, grief – when he heard his brothers and sisters describing things about which he had no knowledge at all.

Then he knew that they saw what he did not see.

Four

He was from the outset of an inquisitive nature, regardless of what he encountered in the finding out of what he did not know, and that cost him much discomfort and trouble. But one incident in particular curbed his curiosity, and filled his heart with a shyness which lingers even yet.

He was sitting down to supper with his father and brothers, and his mother, as was her custom, was superintending the meal and directing the servant and her daughters, who were assisting the servant, in bringing the dishes required for the meal. And he was eating just as the others were eating, when a strange thought occurred to him! What would happen if he took hold of a morsel of food with both hands instead of one as was customary? And what was there to prevent him from making this experiment? Nothing. Lo! he took a morsel in both hands. Then he raised it to his mouth.

At once his brothers burst out laughing. His mother was on the point of tears. His father said in a soft and sorrowful tone, 'That is not the way to eat your food, my son!' And he himself passed a troubled night.

From that time his movements were fettered with infinite caution, fear and shyness. And thenceforth he realised that he had a strong will and also abstained from many kinds of food which he only allowed himself when he was over twenty-five years old. He gave up soup and rice, and all dishes which had to be eaten with spoons because he knew that he could not wield a spoon nicely, and so he didn't want his brothers to laugh at him, his mother to weep or his father to reproach him, albeit softly and sadly.

This incident helped him to understand correctly a traditional story about Abu-l-'Alā.[2]

They say that one day he was eating treacle, some of which, unbeknown to him, fell down the front of his garment. When he went out therefore to lecture to his students, one of them said to him, 'Sir, you have been eating treacle.' Abu-l-'Alā quickly put his hand on his chest and said 'Yes! God save us from gluttony!' Thereafter he gave up eating treacle for the rest of his life.

This incident also led him to appreciate more fully other actions of Abu-l-'Alā. For example he understood the reason why he used to eat unseen by anybody, not even his servant, and that he used to eat in a tunnel under the ground, ordering his servant to lay his meals there and then go away, so that he was left alone with his food and could eat it as he liked.

They also say that one day his students were talking about the melons of Aleppo and saying how excellent they were. Abu-l-'Alā took the trouble to send someone to Aleppo to buy some for them.

When the students ate, the servant kept a piece of melon for his master and put it in the tunnel. But it seems that he did not put it in the place where he usually put the old man's food, and, the latter not liking to ask for his share of the melon, it remained in that place until it went bad and he never tasted it at all.

Our friend understood completely these features of the life of Abu-l-'Alā, because therein he saw himself. How often as a child he used to long to be able to eat by himself, but he never dared communicate this desire to his people. However, he was left alone with portions of the food frequently in the month of Ramadan[3] and at the great festivals of the year, when his family used to partake of various kinds of sweet dishes, such as must be eaten with spoons. Then he used to refuse his portion of them at the table, and his mother, not liking this abstinence of his, would set aside for him a special dish and leave him alone with it in a special room in which he could shut himself up so that nobody was able to see him while he ate.

When at length he reached years of discretion, he made this his general rule. He pursued this course of seclusion when he travelled to Europe for the first time, feigning fatigue and refusing to go to the dining-saloon on board ship, so that food was brought to him in his cabin. Then when he got to France, it was his rule on arrival at a hotel, or when staying with a family, that his food should be brought to him in his room without his bothering to go to the common dining-room. Nor did he abandon this habit until he got married, when his wife broke him of many habits he had grown into.

This incident, again, caused him many kinds of hardship. It made him a by-word among his family and those who knew him before he passed from family life into society.

He was a small eater, not because he had no great appetite, but because he had a horror of being called a glutton or of his brothers winking at one another on account of him. At first this caused him much pain, but it was not long before he got accustomed to it, so that he found it difficult to eat as others ate.

He used to take exceedingly small helpings of food. Now there was an uncle of his who was much vexed with him about it, whenever he saw it, and used to get enraged and rebuke him, urging him to take larger helpings; so that his brothers laughed. This caused him to hate his uncle with a deadly hatred.

He was ashamed to drink at table, fearing that the glass might upset in his hand or that he would take hold of it clumsily when it was handed to him. Therefore he always ate his food dry at the table until such time as he got up and went to wash his hands at the tap, drinking there to his heart's content. Now the water was not always clean, nor was this way of quenching his thirst beneficial to the health. So things went on until he got stomach trouble and no one was able to tell the reason of it.

Moreover, he abstained from all kinds of sports and games, except those which did not give him much trouble, and such as exposed him neither to ridicule nor to sympathy. His favourite was to collect a number of iron rods, take them to a quiet corner of the house, and then put them together, separate them and knock one against the other. Thus he would while away hours until he wearied of it. Then he would fall back on his brothers and friends, who were playing a game in which he would join with his mind but not with his hand. Like that he knew numerous games without ever taking part in them.

Now this abstention of his from play led him to become fond of one kind of diversion, and that was listening to stories and legends. His great delight was to listen to the songs of the bard or the conversation of his father with other men or of his mother with other women, and so he acquired the art of listening. His father and some of his friends were very fond of story-telling. As soon as ever they had finished their afternoon prayers they all collected round one of them, who would recite to them tales of raids and conquests, and of the adventures of Antarah and Zahir Baibars,[4] and narratives about prophets, ascetics and pious folk; and he would read them books of sermons and the religious law.

Our friend would sit at a respectful distance from them, and although they were oblivious of his presence, he was in no way unmindful of what he heard or even of the impression these stories made upon the audience. So it was that when the sun set, people went to their food, but as soon as they had said their evening prayers they assembled again and conversed for a great part of the night. Then came the bard and began to recite the deeds of the Hilalies and Zanaties to him, and our friend would sit listening during the early part of the night just as he did toward the close of the day.

The women in the villages of Egypt do not like silence, nor have they any talent for it, so that if one of them is by herself and cannot find anyone to talk she will divert herself with various kinds of speech; if glad, she will sing, and if she is sad by reason of bereavement she will lament the deceased; for every woman in

Egypt can mourn when she wishes. Best of all when they are by themselves do the village women like to recall their troubles and eulogise those who have departed this life and very often this eulogising causes them to shed real tears.

Our friend was the happiest of mortals when he was listening to his sisters singing or his mother lamenting. However, the song of his sisters used to annoy him and left no impression on him because he found it inane and pointless, without rhyme or reason, whereas the lamentations of his mother used to move him very much and often reduced him to tears. Somewhat after this fashion our friend learnt by heart many songs, many lamentations and many tales both serious and amusing. He learnt something else which had no connection at all with this, to wit passages of the Quran which his old blind grandfather used to recite morning and evening.

This grandfather of his was to him an unattractive and odious person, who used to spend every winter at the house. He became pious and ascetic when life drove him to it, and so he used to pray the regular five times a day and the mention of God was incessantly on his tongue. He would get up toward the end of the night in order to recite the collect for the dawn and would sleep at a belated hour after the evening prayer and recite all manner of collects and prayers.

Now our friend slept in a room adjoining that of the old man and thus could hear him intoning and learn by heart what he intoned, so that he memorised a great number of these collects and prayers.

Moreover, the people of the village were very fond of Sufism[5] and used to perform the zikr. Our friend liked this propensity of theirs because he enjoyed the zikr and the incantations of the chanters during it.

So it was that before he was nine years old he had accumulated a very fair collection of songs, lamentations, stories, poems about the Hilalies and Zanaties, collects, prayers and dervish incantations, and learnt them by heart, and in addition to all that he had learnt the Quran,

Five

Strange to relate, he does not know how he memorised the Quran, nor how he began it, nor how he went over it a second time, although of his life in the village school he remembers numerous episodes, many of which make him laugh even now, while others sadden him.

He recalls the time when he used to go to school carried on the shoulder of one of his brothers because the school was a long way away and he was too weak to go such a distance on foot.

He cannot remember, either, when he began to go to the village school. He sees himself in the early part of the day sitting on the ground in front of 'Our Master', surrounded by a collection of shoes, with some of which he was playing, and he remembers how patched they were. Now 'Our Master' sat on a small, wooden dais that was neither particularly high nor particularly low; it stood on the right of the door as you came in, so that everyone who entered passed 'Our Master'. As soon as 'Our Master' entered the school, it was his custom to take off his cloak, or more accurately his overcoat, and having rolled it up into the shape of a cushion he put it on his right side. Then he would take off his shoes and, sitting cross-legged on his dais, light a cigarette and begin to call the roll.

Now 'Our Master' never discarded his shoes until it was absolutely necessary. He used to patch them on the right side and on the left and on the top and the bottom. Whenever one of his shoes needed patching he would call one of the boys of the school, and taking the shoe in his hand say to him, 'You will go to the cobbler who lives near by and say to him, "Our Master says that this shoe needs a patch on the right side. Look, do you see? Here where I put my finger." The cobbler will reply, "Yes I will patch it." Then you will say to him, "Our Master says that you must choose a strong, coarse, new piece of leather and that you must put it on neatly so that it is invisible or nearly so." He will reply, "Yes I will do that." Then you will say to him, "Our Master says that he is an old customer of yours, so please take that into account," and whatever he says to you don't agree to pay more than a piastre. Now go and come back again in the twinkling of an eye.'

So the boy would depart and 'Our Master' would forget all about him. By the time that he did return, 'Our Master' would have twinkled his eye times without number.

Nevertheless, although this man opened and shut his eye, he could not see anything, or at any rate very little, for he was completely blind except for the faintest glimmer of sight in one eye, so that he could discern shapes without being able to distinguish between them. Not but what he was very pleased with this dim sight of his, and deceived himself into imagining that he could see as well as other people. However, this did not prevent him from relying on two of his pupils to guide him on his way to and from the school, putting an arm on the shoulder of each.

Thus they would proceed three abreast along the street, which they occupied to the detriment of other pedestrians, who had to make way for them. Strange indeed was the sight of 'Our Master' on his way to the school or his house in the morning and evening. He was a bulky, corpulent man and his overcoat increased his bulk. As we mentioned above he put his arms over the shoulders of his two companions, and as the three of them marched along, the earth resounded beneath their tread.

Now 'Our Master' used to choose the most intelligent of his pupils, and those with the best voices, for this important task. This was because he was fond of singing and liked to give singing lessons to his pupils. He would deliver his lesson to them all along the street. Thus he would sing, and at times his companions would begin to accompany him (in song) or merely listen to him at others; or one of them he would charge to sing, and 'Our Master' and his other companion would accompany him.

'Our Master' did not sing with his voice and tongue alone, but with his head and body also. He used to nod his head up and down and waggle it from side to side. Moreover he sang with his hands also, beating time upon the chests of his two companions with his fingers. Sometimes when the song was particularly agreeable to him, and he found that walking did not suit him, he would stop till it was finished. The best of it was that 'Our Master' thought he had a very beautiful voice, though our friend does not think that God ever created an uglier voice than his.

Whenever he read the verse: 'Verily the most unpleasant sound is the braying of asses,' he invariably thought of 'Our Master' while he was beating time to the verses of the Al-Burda[6] on his way to the mosque to pray at noon or on his way home to the house from the school.

Our friend pictures himself, as described above, sitting on the ground playing with the shoes around him, while 'Our Master' hears him recite Surat-ar-Rahman, but he cannot remember whether he was reciting it for the first time or the second.

Indeed on another occasion he sees himself sitting not on the floor among the shoes, but on the right of 'Our Master' on another long dais, and the latter is hearing him recite: 'Do ye enjoin good works on others and yourselves forget to do them? Do ye read the book and then do not understand?' To the best of his belief he had finished reciting the Quran through once and was beginning to do it a second time.

It is not to be wondered at that our friend forgets how he learnt the Quran, since at the time of its completion he was not nine years old. He remembers very clearly the day on which he concluded his study of the Quran, and 'Our Master' telling him some days before, how pleased his father would be with him and how he would make his stipulations for it and demand his past dues. For had he not taught four of our friend's brothers before him, of whom one had gone to Al-Azhar[7] and the others to various schools? So that our friend was the fifth. ... Did 'Our Master' not have many claims upon the family?

These claims 'Our Master' always detailed in terms of food, drink, clothes and money.

The first of all of these dues, of which he would demand payment, when our friend had finished the Quran, would be a rich supper; then a gown and caftan, a pair of shoes, a Maghraby tarbush,[8] a cotton cap of the material of which turbans are made

15

and a golden guinea – he would not be satisfied with anything less than that . . . if they did not pay him all this, he would disown the family and would not take anything from them. Nor would he have any more to do with them. This he swore with the most binding oaths.

It was Wednesday, and 'Our Master' had announced in the morning that our friend would conclude the Quran that day. They set forth in the afternoon, 'Our Master' leading the way supported by his two companions, and behind him our friend, led by one of the orphans in the village. At last they reached the house and 'Our Master' gave the door a push and uttering the customary cry 'Ya Sattar' (O Veiler), made his way to the guest-room, where was the sheikh, who had just finished his afternoon prayers and was reciting some private prayers as was his wont. He greeted them smilingly and confidently. His voice was soft and that of 'Our Master' raucous. Meanwhile our friend said nothing and the orphan was smiling from ear to ear.

The sheikh signed to 'Our Master' and his two companions to be seated, and placed a silver coin in the orphan's hand. Then having called the servant and bidden him take the orphan to a place where he would find something to eat, he patted his son on the head and said 'May God open his ways to you ! Go and tell your mother that "Our Master" is here.'

His mother must have heard the voice of 'Our Master', for she had prepared such things as were necessary for an occasion like this : a tall and wide mug of unadulterated sugared water. It was brought to 'Our Master' and he gulped it down. His two companions also drank two mugs of sugared water. Then coffee was brought and then 'Our Master' urged the sheikh to examine the lad in the Quran, but the sheikh replied 'Leave him to play. He is yet young.' 'Our Master' got up to go, whereupon the sheikh said 'We will say the sunset prayer together, if God wills,' which was of course an invitation to supper.

I cannot recollect that 'Our Master' received any other reward in return for our friend completing the Quran, for he had known the family twenty years and received presents from them regularly, and did not stand on ceremony with them. Indeed he was confident that if he was unlucky with the family this time, he would not be so unlucky some other time.

Six

From that day our small friend was a sheikh, although he was barely nine years old, because he had learnt the Quran by heart; for who memorises the Quran is a sheikh whatever age he be.

His father called him sheikh, his mother called him sheikh, and 'Our Master' used to call him sheikh in front of his parents. He also used to do so either when he was pleased with him or wanted to ask some favour of him. But apart from that he used to call him by his name and very often merely 'kid'.

Now our youthful sheikh was short, thin, pale and rather shabby. He had none of the dignity of sheikhs, and neither a large nor a small part of their reverent demeanour. Moreover his parents contented themselves with magnifying and exalting him by this epithet, which they attached to his name more out of pride and satisfaction with themselves than with the idea of pleasing or petting him.

As for himself, the epithet pleased him at first, but he expected something else, some outward and visible form of reward and encouragement.

He expected to become a real sheikh, and so don a turban and wear a gown and caftan, hence it was difficult to convince him that he was too small to carry a turban on his head or to get into a caftan.

How should he be convinced of it when he was a sheikh who had memorised the Quran ! How could one so young be a sheikh ! How could one who had memorised the Quran be so young ! He was therefore unjustly treated . . . and what greater injustice could there be than that which came between him and his right to the turban, gown and caftan. . . .

It was not many days ere he became disgusted with the title of sheikh and hated to be called by it. He felt that life was full of injustice and deceit, and that mankind (including his parents) wronged him since parenthood did not prevent mothers and fathers from falsehood, trickery and deception.

This feeling soon gave place to one of contempt for the title of sheikh, and the feeling that his father and mother were full of pride and self-admiration. Then it was not long before he forgot all this together with other things.

If the truth were known he was not worthy to be called sheikh, and in spite of his having learnt the Quran by heart he was only worthy to go to the village school as before, shabbily attired, with a cotton cap on his head that was only cleaned once a week, and wearing shoes that were renewed only once a year and not discarded until they were utterly worn out. Then he abandoned them and walked barefoot for a week or several weeks until God permitted him to have a new pair.

All this he richly deserved, because his knowledge of the Quran was not of long duration. . . . Was he alone to blame for that or was the blame equally divided between him and 'Our Master'? The truth was that 'Our Master' neglected him for a time, and concentrated his attention on others who had not yet finished the Quran. He neglected him in order to take a rest and also because he had not been paid for our friend's finishing the Quran.

Our friend rather enjoyed this neglect and began going to the village school and spending the entire day there in complete rest and uninterrupted play, waiting for the end of the year. Then his brother at Al-Azhar would come from Cairo, and when his holiday had come to an end, return to Cairo, taking our friend with him to become a sheikh in very truth and to study at Al-Azhar.

Months passed in this way. Our friend used to go to the village school and return from it without having done any work, confident that he had learnt the Quran by heart, while 'Our Master' was equally assured that he had learnt the Quran until the fatal day . . . and it certainly was a fatal day, in which for the first time our friend tasted the bitterness of failure, humiliation, degradation and hatred of life.

He returned from the school in the afternoon of that day, calm and self-assured, but he had hardly entered the house before his father called him, addressing him by the title of sheikh. He went to him and found him with two of his friends. His father came to meet him, bade him sit down in gentle tones and asked him some customary questions.

Then he asked him to recite 'The Sura of the Poets'. This request fell on him like a thunderbolt. He began to reflect and meditate. He uttered the customary phrase, 'I take refuge with God from the accursed Satan,' and also 'In the name of God the Beneficent, the Merciful,' but after that all he could remember of 'The Sura of the Poets' was that it was one of the three that begin with Ta Sin Mim,[9] so he began to repeat Ta Sin Mim over and over again, without being able to arrive at what came after it. His father prompted him by telling him some of the words which followed, but in spite of that he could not proceed at all. So his father said, 'Recite the Sura of the Ant, then.' Now he remembered that this Sura, like that of the Poets, began with Ta Sin Mim and he began to repeat this phrase. Again his father helped him, but he could not make any progress. . . . So his father said 'Read the Sura of the Stories, then.' He remembered that this was the third that began with Ta Sin Mim and he began to repeat it again, but this time his father did not prompt him at all. Instead he said quietly, 'Go ! I thought that you had learnt the Quran?'

Our friend stood ashamed while the perspiration poured forth. Meanwhile the two men began to make excuses for him on account of shyness and his tender age. So he went away wondering whether to blame himself because he had forgotten the Quran, or 'Our Master' for neglecting him or his father because he had examined him.

Whatever it was, the evening of this day was indeed a black one. He did not appear at the supper-table, and his father did not ask where he was. His mother came and asked him somewhat reluctantly to have supper with her, but he refused, so she left him, and he went to sleep.

On the whole this hateful evening was preferable to the morrow when he went to the village school, for then 'Our Master' called him roughly, 'What happened yesterday? How was it you were unable to recite the Sura of the Poets? Have you really forgotten it? Recite it to me!'

So our friend began to recite Ta Sin Mim. . . . It was the same story as had happened with his father the day before.

'Our Master' exclaimed, 'May God reward me well for all the time I have spent with you and for all the effort I have expended on your instruction, so you have forgotten the Quran and must learn it again. Not that I am to blame, nor you, but only your father; for if he had paid me my dues on the day you finished the Quran, then God would have blessed him by causing you to remember it, but he denied me my just dues, and so God has driven the Quran out of your head!'

Then he began to go through the Quran with him from the beginning, just as he did with those who were not sheikhs or had not learnt the Quran.

Seven

There is no doubt that he learnt the Quran thoroughly after that in a very short time. He remembers that he returned from the village school on a certain day with 'Our Master', and on this day 'Our Master' made a point of going home with him. When they reached the house 'Our Master' bent and pushed the door, which opened to him. Then he uttered his familiar cry 'Ya Sattar!' (O Veiler!) The sheikh was in the guest-room as usual, and had just said the afternoon prayer. When 'Our Master' had seated himself, he said to the sheikh, 'So you averred that your son had forgotten the Quran and blamed me severely for that! Now I swore to you that he had not forgotten but was only nervous, but you contradicted me and mocked my beard. I have come to-day that you may put your son to a test in my presence, and I swear that should it appear that he has not learnt the Quran, I will shave off this beard of mine and become a laughing-stock among the fuqaha[10] in this town!' The sheikh replied, 'Don't get excited. Wouldn't it have been better to say "Well, he forgot the Quran, so I have been through it with him again"?' Said 'Our Master', 'I swear by God three times that he did not forget it, nor have I been through it with him again. I only heard him recite the Quran and he recited it to me like flowing water, neither stopping nor hesitating.'

Our friend listened to this dispute, knowing full well that his father was right and that 'Our Master' was lying, but he said nothing and stood waiting for the examination.

The examination was a very severe one, but on this occasion our friend was smart and intelligent, answering every question that was put to him without hesitation. Indeed he recited so quickly that his father said, 'Not so fast – it is a sin to gabble the Quran!' When at last he had finished, his father said to him, 'Well done! Go to your mother and tell her that you have really learnt the Quran this time.'

He went to his mother, but said nothing to her, nor did she ask him any questions.

On that day when 'Our Master' departed, he took with him a gown of broadcloth which the sheikh had presented to him.

Eight

On the morrow 'Our Master' came to school in the best of spirits. He addressed the lad by the title of sheikh on this occasion, saying, 'You certainly deserve to be called sheikh to-day, for yesterday you raised up my head, caused my face to shine and honoured my beard. Moreover your father was obliged to give me the gown. Yesterday you recited the Quran like streams of gold, while I was on fire fearing lest you should slip or go wrong. In fact I commended you to the Alive, the Eternal, who slumbers not nor sleeps, until the examination was over. To-day I will excuse you from recitation, but I want to make a covenant with you. You must promise me that you will keep it.' The lad replied modestly, 'Certainly I will keep it.' 'Then,' said 'Our Master', 'give me your hand,' and so saying he took hold of the lad's hand. Next the lad felt something strange in his hand, which terrified him, the like of which he had never felt before; something broad that waggled and was full of hair, into which his fingers sank.

In fact 'Our Master' had put his beard into the lad's hand, saying, 'This is my beard by which I adjure you, and which I enjoin you not to despise. Therefore say "By God Almighty" three times and by the truth of the Glorious Quran I will not despise it.' So the lad swore as 'Our Master' wished, and when he had finished the oath, 'Our Master' asked, 'Into how many parts is the Quran divided?' He replied, 'Thirty.' 'How many days do you work at school?' asked 'Our Master'. 'Five,' replied the lad. 'Then if you wished to read the Quran once a week how many parts would you have to read a day?' The lad pondered for a moment and then he said, 'Six parts.' 'Then swear that you will recite six parts of the Quran every working day to the 'Arif,[11] and that you will begin this recitation, as soon as ever you come to school in the morning, When you have finished your daily portion, you will be free to play and amuse yourself as you like, provided you do not distract the other lads from their tasks.' . . .

The lad took this covenant upon himself and 'Our Master', having called the 'Arif, made him swear a similar oath, namely to hear the lad recite his six parts of the Quran daily. Moreover he entrusted to him his honour, the regard for his beard and the reputation of the school in the town, and the 'Arif accepted the trust. So terminated this spectacle, at which the pupils of the school assisted with wonder.

Nine

From that time the lad's educational connection with 'Our Master' was terminated, and he passed into the charge of the 'Arif.

Now this 'Arif was no less strange an individual than 'Our Master'. He was a tall, slender youth and black as coal, the offspring of a Sudanese father and a mulatto woman.

He was most unlucky, since he was unsuccessful in every useful undertaking in life. He had tried every kind of trade, without being able to master one. His father sent him to numerous craftsmen to learn their trades, but he did not succeed in doing so; then he tried to find him work in a sugar factory, as a workman or a watchman or a doorkeeper or a servant, but he was not a success at any of these jobs.

After that his father became embittered and began to hate and despise him. He showed preference to his brothers, who were all working and earning money.

Now he had been to the village school in his boyhood. There he had learnt to read and write, and had memorised some suras of the Quran, which he soon forgot. So that when he was in sore straits, he betook himself to 'Our Master' in his extremity and complained to him of his plight. 'Our Master' said 'Come here and be 'Arif. It will be your duty to teach reading and writing to the lads, to supervise them and prevent them from playing, and to take my place when I am absent. I will go through the Quran with them and make them learn it. It will also be your duty to open the school before the sun rises and to see to the cleaning of the place before the pupils come. You will have to lock up the school after the afternoon prayer, take the keys, and generally speaking be my right hand. In return you shall have a quarter of the cash profits of the school, and that will be paid to you every week or every month.'

Thus the agreement was made between the two men, and having both recited the opening chapter[12] of the Quran over it the 'Arif began his labours.

Now the 'Arif bitterly detested 'Our Master', and despised him, although he used to flatter him.

At the same time 'Our Master' disliked the 'Arif intensely and despised him, but used to flatter him also to his face.

The 'Arif hated 'Our Master' because he was a marked cheat and liar; he used to hide from the 'Arif some of the profits of the school, and appropriated to himself the best of the food that the pupils brought with them. He despised him because although he was blind he pretended he could see, and also because, although his voice was hideous, he pretended it was beautiful.

And as for 'Our Master', he hated the 'Arif because he was cunning and crafty, hiding from him much that he ought to tell him about, and because he was a thief and stole what was brought for both of them at lunch-time, reserving special dainties for himself. Also because he conspired with the bigger boys of the school and played with them behind 'Our Master's' back. Then after the afternoon prayer, when the school had been locked up, there were meetings between him and them under the mulberry tree or at the bridge or at the sugar factory.

The strangest thing was that the two men were both perfectly right, but, in spite of their mutual hatred and exasperation, they were obliged to help one another, the one in order to obtain a livelihood and the other because he needed someone to manage the affairs of the school for him.

So it was that our lad began his connection with the 'Arif and started to read six sections of the Quran every day. This arrangement, however, did not last three days, for the lad got tired of it on the first day, the 'Arif on the second, and on the third day they revealed to each other their mutual boredom.

On the fourth day it was agreed that the lad should recite the six sections to himself in the presence of the 'Arif until he found some difficulty or an expression of which he was not sure, when he would ask the 'Arif about it.

So the lad would come to school every morning, salute the 'Arif, sit upon the ground in front of him and begin to move his lips, murmuring the while as though he were reciting the Quran. Periodically he would question the 'Arif about some word, and the latter would at times answer and at others ignore him. 'Our Master' used to come every day a little before noon and when he had said good morning and sat down, his first concern was to call the lad and ask 'Have you recited?' 'Yes.' 'From where to where?' Then the lad would reply, 'From "The Cow" to "Verily thou shalt find" on Saturday, and from "Verily thou shalt find" to "Ma Ubarry" (I do not acquit) on Sunday ...' and in this way he divided up the Quran into the six parts agreed upon by jurists of religious law, for every day of the five he set aside one part in particular to quote to 'Our Master' when he questioned him.

Nevertheless the 'Arif was not satisfied with this agreement which was so restful alike to him and the lad.

In addition he wished to profit from the position of the lad in his charge, and so he used to warn him occasionally that he would tell 'Our Master' that some chapters of the Quran, such as the Sura of Hud[13] or Surat-Al-Anbia (The chapter of the prophets) or Surat-Al-Ahzab (The chapter of the parties) were not properly learnt; moreover since the whole of the Quran had not been properly learnt by the lad because he had neglected his recitation for a month, he hated to be examined by 'Our Master' and therefore bought the silence of the 'Arif by every possible means, frequently handing over to him pocketfuls of bread or pastry or dried dates.

Frequently too did he pay him the piastre which his father used to give him from time to time, and which he wished to spend on peppermint 'bull's-eyes'.

Many a time he got round his mother to give him a large piece of sugar, so that when he got to the school he might hand it over to the 'Arif, although he himself coveted the whole or a part of it.

The 'Arif would take it and having called for some water, dip the sugar in it. Next he proceeded to suck it with zest, finally swallowing it when the sugar was melted or nearly melted. ... Many a time too he denied himself the food which was brought from the house to the school for him every day at noon, in spite of being ravenously hungry, so that the 'Arif might eat instead of him and not tell 'Our Master' that he had not learnt the Quran properly.

Nevertheless these continued favours soon secured for him the affection of the 'Arif, who made friends with him and began to accompany him to the Mosque after lunch to attend the noonday prayers.

Gradually he began to trust him and to confide in him. He requested him to be allowed to read the Quran with some pupils and to hear the recitation of others who had begun to learn it or were reciting it a second time.

Here our friend pursued exactly the same course as the 'Arif had pursued with him.

He used to sit in front of the pupils and, having set them a passage to recite, pass the time in conversation with his friends. When at length he had finished his conversation, he would turn to them, and if he perceived any playing or slacking or disturbance among them, there would ensue a warning, followed by abuse and blows, and lastly a report to the 'Arif.

The truth was that he did not know the Quran better than his pupils, but the 'Arif had adopted this procedure with him, so that he was obliged to become a veritable 'Arif himself. And if the 'Arif did not abuse him or beat him or report him to 'Our Master', that was because he had paid dearly for all that.

The pupils understood this and began to pay dearly too, and he began to take bribes to the extent of what he paid the 'Arif. However, his bribes were of various kinds. Since he was never stinted at home, he had no need of bread or dried dates or sugar. Nor could he accept money, since he could not spend it alone, for if he did accept it, he would give himself away and fall into disgrace. Therefore he became a hard taskmaster and difficult to please, so that the pupils taxed their brains to gain his favour and bought him peppermints, sugar-candy, melon-seeds and monkey nuts, much of which he used to present to the 'Arif.

One kind of bribery in particular he found most entertaining and diverting and it caused him to neglect his duty shamefully. This kind was of stories, tales and books. If any pupil could tell him a story or buy him a volume from the man who travelled round the villages hawking books, or could recite to him an episode from the story of 'Alzir Salim' or 'Abu Zaid', he might be sure of anything he wished in the way of favour, companionship and partiality.

The most skilful of his pupils in this respect was a little blind girl called Nafisa.[14] Her people had sent her to the village school to learn the Quran, and when she had done this satisfactorily, 'Our Master' gave her into the charge of the 'Arif, who in turn entrusted her to our friend, and he treated her in the same way as the 'Arif had treated him.

The family of this young lady were well-to-do, in fact *nouveaux riches*, her father having risen from donkey man to wealthy merchant, who spent money on his family without stint and bestowed upon them every comfort in life. Consequently Nafisa was never without money and was, therefore, the best able to choose bribes.

She was also the best story-teller and the most inventive, and knew more kinds of merry songs and heart-rending dirges than any of them, being equally adept at singing and lamentation. She was capricious and rather eccentric.

So it was that most of our friend's time was occupied in listening to her conversation, lamentations and stories, and accepting various kinds of bribes from her; and while our friend was engaged in giving and taking bribes, and in deceiving and being deceived, the Quran was steadily effaced from his mind verse by verse and chapter by chapter until dawned the inevitable day ... and O what a day it was !

Ten

It was Wednesday and our friend had spent the day pleasantly and happily. He averred to 'Our Master' first thing in the morning that he had finished the last part of the Quran, after which he was free to listen to tales and anecdotes and to play for the rest of the day.

When he left the school he did not go home directly, but went with a company of friends to the Mosque to say the afternoon prayers. Now he used to like going to the Mosque, climbing up the minaret and taking part with the muezzin in the 'taslim', which is the call which follows the ceremonial call to prayer.

On this day he went to the Mosque, climbed up the minaret, took part in the call to prayer and prayed. Then he thought to return home but found he had lost his shoes, and could not find them anywhere. He had put them down by the side of the mina-ret, but when he had finished his prayers he went to get them and lo! they had been stolen. This caused him some small annoy-ance, but he was happy and cheerful that day, so he did not worry or reckon how great would be the consequence. He re-turned to the house barefoot and although it was a considerable distance from the Mosque to the house, that did not alarm him as he often walked barefoot.

As soon as he entered the house, the sheikh, who was in the guest-room as was his custom, called out to him, 'Where are your shoes?' To which he replied, 'I forgot them and left them at school.' The sheikh paid no attention to this reply and took no notice of the lad as he came in, so that he began to talk to his mother and sisters for a little, and to eat a piece of bread as he did every day when he returned from the school.

At length the sheikh called him and he hastened in response. When he had settled down in his place, his father said to him, 'What have you read to-day of the Quran?' He answered that having read the last six parts, he had finished it. The sheikh said, 'Do you still know it properly?' He replied, 'Yes.' 'Then recite the Sura of Sheba to me.' Now our friend had forgotten the Sura of Sheba together with all the other suras, nor did God help him at all. The sheikh said, 'Well, recite the Sura of the Creator'. Still God did not help him to speak. So the sheikh said gently and mock-ingly, 'You averred that you still knew the Quran properly. All right, recite Surat Yasin.' God helped him to recite the first verses of this sura, but after that he became tongue-tied, and the saliva in his mouth dried up. A terrible quivering took hold of him, fol-lowed by cold sweat pouring down his face.

Then the sheikh said quietly, 'Get up! Try not to forget your shoes every day. As far as I can see you have lost them just as you have lost your knowledge of the Quran. However, I have to deal with "Our Master" in a different fashion.'

The lad went out of the guest-room with head cast down, stumbling in his dismay, until he reached the 'karar' or larder, which is the room in a house where various kinds of food are kept and pigeons are bred. In one corner was the 'qirma', which is a big thick block of wood, like a tree-trunk, on which his mother cut the meat.

Now lying on this block was a collection of knives of all sorts, long and short, heavy and light.

Our friend then went to the larder, made for the corner in which was the block and reaching out for the chopper which was the bulkiest, sharpest and heaviest weapon there, took it in his right hand and let the edge fall on the back of his neck!

Then he uttered a cry and the chopper fell from his hand.

His mother, who was near at hand and had taken no notice of him when he passed her, rushed to him while he stood there in distress with the blood flowing from the back of his neck and the chopper lying at his side. She quickly threw a glance at the wound and as quickly saw that it was not serious, and she did nothing else but pour down on him abuse, blame and reproach.

Then, catching hold of one of his hands she dragged him into the kitchen and having simply thrown him down in a corner, went on with her work.

There our friend lay without moving or speaking or crying or even thinking, just as if he were nothing at all. Meanwhile his brothers and sisters played and made a noise round about him, but took no notice of him; nor did he take any notice of them.

Evening drew on and in due course he was summoned to answer to his father. So he went out, ashamed, and stumblingly entered the guest-room. But before his father could ask him anything 'Our Master' forestalled him with this question: 'Did you not read six sections of the Quran to me to-day?' 'Yes,' he replied. 'Did you not read the Sura of Sheba to me yesterday?' 'Yes,' he replied. 'Then why cannot you recite it to me to-day?' He did not answer. 'Recite the Sura of Sheba,' ordered 'Our Master', but the Lord opened not his lips to the extent of even one word. 'Recite "The Sagda",' said his father, but he could not do any better.

At this point the sheikh became very angry, but with 'Our Master', not with the lad, and he said, 'There, you see; he goes to school not to recite and learn, not for you to take care of him or pay any attention to him, but only to play and idle away his time. He returned to-day barefoot and averred that he had forgotten his shoes and left them at school. .... I don't think your concern for his learning the Quran is any greater than your concern as to whether he walks barefoot or shod. ....'

'Our Master' replied, 'I swear by God three times that I have not neglected him for a single day, and if only I had not left the school to-day before the departure of the pupils, he would never have returned barefoot. Indeed he has been reciting the Quran to me once every week; every day six portions, which I have heard as soon as ever I come to the school in the morning.' The sheikh said, 'I do not believe any of this.' 'Our Master' expostulated, 'May my wife be thrice divorced! I swear I have never lied to you, nor am I lying now. Assuredly I have heard him recite the Quran once every week.' 'I don't believe it,' was the sheikh's retort. 'Do you think that the money you pay to me every month is more precious to me than my wife?' asked 'Our Master'; 'Or do you think that for the sake of what you pay me I should make lawful what is unlawful and live with a wife I have divorced three times in your presence?' 'That is something that does not concern me,' replied the sheikh, 'but from now on the lad will not go to school.' So saying he got up and went out, and 'Our Master' also got up and took his departure very despondently.

As for our friend, he remained in his place reflecting neither on the Quran nor on what had taken place, but only on 'Our Master's' capacity for falsehood and this threefold divorce which he had flung out as carelessly as he might have flung a cigarette on the ground when he had finished smoking it!

The lad did not appear at the supper table. In fact for three days he avoided both his father's presence and the dining-room. However, on the fourth day his father came to him in the kitchen where he liked to sit apart next to the oven, and began to talk to him good-humouredly, kindly and sympathetically, until the lad responded and began to cheer up after his sulkiness.

Then his father took him by the hand, led him to his seat at the dinner table and paid special attention to him during lunch.

When the lad had finished eating and got up to go, his father said to him a sentence in cruel jest, which he has never forgotten because it made all his brothers laugh at him and because they remembered it against him and used to tease him afterwards with it from time to time.

The sentence was: 'Have you learnt the Quran?'

Eleven

So the lad ceased going to the school and 'Our Master' stopped coming to the house. The sheikh found another faqih to come to the house every day and read there a sura of the Quran in the place of 'Our Master', and made the lad read for an hour or two, and then he continued to be free to amuse himself and play in the house as soon as the new schoolmaster had taken his departure.

In the late afternoon his friends and companions used to visit him on their way back from the school and narrate to him what happened in the school. He enjoyed that and used to make fun of them and their school and 'Our Master' and the 'Arif, for he imagined that he had finished for ever with the village school and everybody connected with it; that he would never return to it nor see the schoolmaster or the 'Arif again.

So he gave his tongue full rein and spoke about the two men without restraint. He began to expose such of their faults and mis-doings as he had previously kept to himself. He began to run them down in front of the pupils, characterising them as lying, dishonest and covetous. He used to talk about them in an abominable fashion, thereby easing his own feelings and at the same time providing pleasure for the boys.

Indeed, why should he not talk freely about the two men, when there was only a month before he would be going to Cairo? His brother the Azharite would return home from Cairo in a few days and when he had spent his holiday he would take our friend back with him to Al-Azhar, where he would become a student,[15] and where he would be cut off from all news of the schoolmaster and the 'Arif.

31

The truth was that he was happy in these days and felt a certain superiority over his friends and contemporaries. For he did not go to the school as they did, but the schoolmaster had to come to him, and he was going to Cairo where were Al-Azhar and Sayyidunal-Hussein (Our Lord Hussein) and Sayyida Zainab[16] (Lady Zainab) and other saints. Nor was Cairo to him anything other than the seat of Al-Azhar and the shrines of saints and pious folk.

But this happiness was to be followed by bitter disillusionment. The reason of this was that 'Our Master' could not bear this severance patiently, nor was he able to endure the triumph of Shaikh Abdul-Gawwad over him, and so he began to entreat the favour of the sheikh through the medium of so-and-so and so-and-so. Surely enough the sheikh relented and ordered the lad to return to the school next morning. . . .

He returned, much to his disgust, calculating what he would meet at the hands of 'Our Master' in the course of his reading the Quran for the third time with him. But the matter did not rest at that, for the pupils had been carrying all that they had heard from their friend to the schoolmaster and the 'Arif.

What a time our friend had in the luncheon-hour all that week! What with the reproaches he got from 'Our Master' and what with the 'Arif repeating to him expressions which his tongue had uttered on the assumption of never seeing the two men again.

During that week the lad learnt to bridle his tongue and he also learnt how mistaken and foolish it is to put any confidence in the promises of men and the way they treat solemn covenants. For did not the sheikh swear that the lad should not return to the school? and lo! he had returned. What then was the difference between the sheikh swearing and breaking his oath? and 'Our Master' glibly making use of divorce and solemn oath when all the time he knew he was lying? And these boys who used to talk to him abusing the schoolmaster and the 'Arif and at the same time inciting him to abuse them, so that when they had succeeded in making him do so, they might curry favour with the two men using him as a means thereto; and then again his mother who used to laugh at him and incite 'Our Master' against him when he came to her with tales about 'Our Master' that these pupils had brought him; and his brothers, who used to gloat over him and repeat to him the saying of 'Our Master' from time to time to tease him and arouse his indignation.

But he bore it all with patience and endurance. Why should he not be patient and endure it when his departure from all this environment was only a month or less away?

Twelve

Nevertheless when the month had passed and the Azharite had returned to Cairo, our friend was still in the same position, not having either gone to Cairo, or donned a turban, or put on a gown and caftan. He was yet young and it was not possible for him to be sent to Cairo.

Moreover, his brother did not want to be bothered with him, and so he advised that he should stay where he was for another year. So he stayed behind and no one cared whether he was pleased or angry.

But his mode of life was to be different to some extent, for his brother the Azharite had advised that he should spend the year in preparation for Al-Azhar, and had given him two books, one of which he was to learn in its entirety and of the other he was only to master various pages.

The book which he had to learn by heart was the Alfiyya of Ibn Malik,[17] and the other book was a collection of texts. The Azharite, before his departure, charged him to begin by learning the Alfiyya and, when he had finished it and was absolutely certain of it, to learn certain unfamiliar things from the other book; various parts of which were called the Al-Jawhara, the Al-Kharida, the Al-Sirajiyya, the Al-Rahbiyya, and Lamiat-al-Af'al.

These names aroused feelings of pride and awe in the breast of the lad, because he did not understand the meaning of them and

33

because he supposed that they indicated learning; also because he knew that his Azharite brother had learnt them, and having understood them had become learned.

Moreover, his brother had attained this distinguished position in the estimation of his parents, brothers and all the people of the village. Did they not all talk about his return a month beforehand? And when he did come they flocked to him joyfully, anxious to do him every kindness. Did not his father drink in his words and repeat them to people with pride and joy? Did not the villagers beseech him to deliver them a lecture on the Unity or Jurisprudence?[18] And what might the Unity be? And what might the Jurisprudence be? Then again, did not the sheikh beg and implore him, making the most extravagant promises and pledging what he could fulfil and also what he could not, all that his son might preach the Friday sermon to the people?

And on this memorable day, the Prophet's birthday, what a lot of honour and respect, reverence and magnification the Azharite received! They had bought him a new caftan, a new gown, a new tarbush and new slippers, and had talked about this day, and what would happen on it, days before.

Wherefore when at last the day arrived and was half spent, the family hastened to their food and partook meagrely of it; the Azharite youth put on his new clothes, donned a green turban for the occasion and threw a Kashmir shawl round his shoulders. His mother prayed and invoked the protection of God upon him, while his father went out and came in again in his pleasure and excitement.

At length, when the youth had completed his toilet and was satisfied with his own appearance, he went out and found a horse waiting for him at the door. Willing hands lifted him and placed him in the saddle, and people surrounded him to right and left, while others went in front of him and again others walked behind. Rifles were fired into the air and women ululated on every side.

The air was laden with the perfume of incense and voices were raised in songs of praise of the Prophet. All this great concourse moved slowly, so that it seemed as though the earth and all the houses on it moved with it.

And all this because the Azharite youth had been chosen caliph, and they must needs march with him in this striking procession through the town and the villages round about. Why was he chosen caliph in place of other youths? Because the Azharite had studied learning and had learnt the Alfiyya by heart and Al-Jawhara and Al-Kharida.

How happy and conceited he was when he went to the school on Saturday morning with a copy of the Alfiyya in his hand! For this copy had raised him many ranks, although it was well worn, dirty and badly bound. Still, in spite of its meanness and dirtiness it was equal in his opinion to fifty copies of the Quran which his fellows carried.

As for the Quran he had learnt its contents by heart and derived no benefit from what he had learnt. Moreover, many youths had learned it by heart and nobody took any notice of them nor were they elected caliphs on the Prophet's birthday.

But the Alfiyya. . . . What does it convey to you? Let it suffice you that 'Our Master' has not learnt a word of it, and also that the 'Arif would be no good at reading the first few verses of it. Besides, the Alfiyya is poetry, and there is no poetry in the Quran.

There was one verse that rejoiced his heart more than anything else and before any chapter in the Quran. It was: 'Thus spake Muhammed, and he's the son of Malik, I praise the Lord God the best possessor.'[19]

Thirteen

How should he not rejoice, when he had felt from the very first day that he had been raised many degrees. 'Our Master' could not supervise his learning of the Alfiyya, nor could he hear him recite it, for the Alfiyya was far beyond the scope of the village school. The lad was required to go to the Religious Law Courts every day to recite to the Qadi those portions of the Alfiyya which he wished him to learn.

Now the Qadi was one of the Ulema of Al-Azhar,[20] far greater than his Azharite brother although his father did not believe that and did not think that the Judge was equal to his son.

Anyhow he was one of the Ulema of Al-Azhar, and a Qadi of the religious law, pronouncing his 'qafs' broadly, and stressing his 'rays'.[21] He was in the Law Courts too, not in the village school. He used to sit on a raised dais covered with carpets and cushions, such as could not be compared with the dais of 'Our Master'. Nor was it surrounded by patched shoes. At his door were two men who acted as ushers and whom people called by a wonderful name not devoid of awe, namely 'Apostles'.

Yes, the lad liked going to the Law Courts every morning and reciting a chapter of the Alfiyya to the Qadi. How magnificently the judge used to recite! How he used to fill his mouth with the 'qaf' and 'ray'! How his voice used to quiver when he recited the words of Ibn Malik:

'Our *kalam* (speech) is significant utterance such as "go straight",
  and would consist of noun, verb and particle.
The singular of it is *kalima* and *qawl* is the least "particular".
By *kalimatun* whereby speech may be meant.'

The Qadi was able to make a great impression on the lad and fill him with humility when he read these verses:

'It induces satisfaction without resentment.
It surpasses the Alfiyya of Ibn Mu'ty;
But he being a pioneer has merit,
And deserves my hearty thanks.
And May God grant abundant gifts
To me and to him in the world to come.'

The Qadi read this in a voice broken with sobs; then he said to the lad, 'He who humbles himself before God, is exalted by Him – do you understand these verses?' The lad replied that he did not. 'Well,' said the Qadi, 'when the author (may God have mercy upon him) began to compose the Alfiyya he became conceited and overtaken by pride, so that he said, "It surpasses the Alfiyya of Ibn Mu'ty." But that night in a dream he saw Ibn Mu'ty, who came and reproached him severely. Therefore when he awoke from his sleep he rectified this self-deceit and said, "But he being a pioneer has merit".'

How happy and joyful the sheikh was when the lad returned home that afternoon and related to him what he had heard from the Qadi, and read to him the first verse of the Alfiyya! He would interrupt him now and then in the middle of these verses, with the word which people use to express approval: 'Allah! Allah!'

But there is a limit to everything, and our friend went on learning the Alfiyya happily enough until he read the chapter on 'Subject and Predicate', and then his energy abated.

His father used to ask him every afternoon if he had gone to the Law Courts and he would reply, 'Yes.' Then his father would say, 'How many verses have you learnt today?' He would reply, 'Twenty.' 'Then recite to me what you have learnt,' his father would say, and he would proceed to do so.

However, it became too hard for him from the chapter on Subject and Predicate onward, so that he used to learn it and go to the Law Courts sluggishly, dawdling as he went. Till at last he reached the chapter on the Cognate Accusative and then he could not make any progress at all. He continued to go to the Law Courts every day, and to read one of the chapters of the Alfiyya to the Qadi until such time as he returned to the school, when he would throw down the Alfiyya in a corner and go off to games, amusement and the reading of stories and anecdotes.

When in the afternoon his father asked him if he had been to the Law Courts, he replied that he had. 'How many verses have you learnt?' 'Twenty.' 'From which chapter?' 'From the chapter on the Genitive or the chapter on the Adjective or the chapter on the broken plural.' Then he would say to him, 'Recite

what you have learnt to me.' And the boy would recite to him
twenty verses from the first two hundred, at one time from the
Declinable and Indeclinable, and at another from the Definite and
Indefinite, and at yet a third time from the Subject and Predicate.

For the sheikh understood nothing of it, and had no notion
that his son was deceiving him. He was quite satisfied as long as
he heard words in the form of verse, and he had confidence in
the Qadi.

The strangest thing was that the sheikh never thought once
of opening the Alfiyya and following the lad while he was reciting. If he had done so one day it would have been the same
story as that of the Sura of the Poets or of Sheba or the Creator,
over again.

But the lad did expose himself to this danger once and had not
his mother interceded for him, there would have been a memorable scene between him and his father.

He had a brother who was at a secular school. This brother
had returned from Cairo to spend his summer holidays at home,
and it happened that he attended the daily examination for
several consecutive days. He heard the sheikh ask the lad 'Which
chapter have you recited?' And the lad replied, 'The chapter on
the Conjunction,' for example, but when he asked him to repeat
it, he repeated the chapter on the Proper Noun or the Relative
Clause and Relative Pronoun.

The young man said nothing on the first day nor on the
following day. But when it happened repeatedly, he waited until
the sheikh had gone and then he said to the lad in front of his
mother, 'You are deceiving your father and lying to him. You
play in the school and don't learn any of the Alfiyya at all.'

The lad replied, 'You are a liar and what has it got to do with
you anyhow? . . . the Alfiyya is for Azharites, not for those in
lay schools! Ask the judge and he will tell you that I go to the
Law Courts.'

The big brother said, 'Which chapter did you learn to-day?'
The lad replied, 'Such and such a chapter.' Said the youth, 'But
you didn't recite that to your father, you only recited such and

such a chapter. Bring a copy of the Alfiyya and I will examine you in it.'

Then the lad was dumbfounded, and his discomfiture was apparent.

The youth was minded to tell the whole story to the sheikh, but his mother besought him not to, and because he was fond of his mother and had compassion on his brother, he said nothing. And so the sheikh remained in ignorance until the Azharite (brother) returned. As soon as he arrived he examined the lad and it was not long before he discovered the true state of affairs. But he was not angry, neither did he warn him nor inform the sheikh. He only ordered the lad to cease going to the school or the Law Courts and made him learn the whole of the Alfiyya in ten days.

Fourteen

Now in the towns and villages of provincial Egypt learning enjoys a prestige the like of which is unknown in the capital and its divers haunts of learning.

Nor is there any great cause for marvel or astonishment at that, for it is simply the law of supply and demand, which is true just as much of learning as of other things, notably buying and selling.

Whereas in Cairo the ulema come and go and no one takes much notice of them; and while the learned speak and speak abundantly, disposing of every kind of subject without anyone in Cairo paying any attention to them except their students, in the provinces you see the learned and sheikhs of the towns and villages coming and going in an atmosphere of majesty and re- spect. When they speak, people listen to them with an esteem that fascinates and attracts.

Our friend came under the influence of this country spirit. He used to magnify the learned just as the country people did, and almost believed that they were created from some pure clay quite distinct from that from which all other people were created. When he used to listen to them speaking, admiration and wonder seized him, of which he tried to find the like in Cairo in the presence of the great ulemas and the majority of the sheikhs, but in vain.

The learned of the town, who shared the admiration and affection of the people, numbered three or four. One of them was a clerk in the religious courts; a short, bulky man with a rough but sonorous voice. He filled the sides of his mouth with his words when he spoke, and these words came out to you bulkily like their speaker, and roughly also like their speaker. The meaning struck you just as the syllables struck you.

Now this sheikh was one who had not been successful at Al-Azhar. He had spent as many years as he had wished there and had failed to get either the degree in learning or the degree in jurisprudence; so he obtained the position of clerk of the courts.

Meanwhile his brother was a distinguished judge and had been given jurisdiction over one of the provinces, and this sheikh could never sit in any assembly without boasting about his brother and running down the judge he himself was with.

He belonged to the Hanafite sect, and the Hanafites in the town were few;[22] in fact, there were scarcely any followers of Abu Hanifa at all. This used to annoy him and enrage him against his opponents among the rest of the ulema, who followed Al-Shafi'y or Malik and who found an echo to their learning, and seekers of their rulings on sacred law, among the townspeople.

So he never missed an opportunity of glorifying the jurisprudence of Abu Hanifa and at the same time disparaging that of Malik and Al-Shafi'y.

The country people are rather cunning and intelligent so that they knew quite well that the sheikh only said what he said and did what he did under the influence of spite and anger. Therefore they sympathised with him and laughed at him.

Between him and the young Azharite there was great rivalry. Every year he was elected caliph, so that it annoyed him that this young man had been elected caliph instead of him. When the people began to talk about the young man delivering the Friday sermon, the sheikh listened and said nothing.

At last Friday came and when the mosque was filled with people, and the young man proceeded to ascend the pulpit, the sheikh stood up, went up to the Imam and addressing him in a voice which all the people could hear, said, 'The youth is yet immature, and it is not seemly that he should ascend the pulpit and preach and lead people in prayer, while among them are sheikhs and men of riper years. If you allow him access to the pulpit, I shall go.' Then he turned to the people and said, 'Whosoever desires that his prayers be not null and void, let him follow me !' When the people heard this, there was a commotion and they were on the point of breaking out into strife, when the Imam stood up, preached to them and prayed with them. So the way was barred between the young man and the pulpit that year. Nevertheless the young man had taken great pains to learn the sermon, had prepared for the event for several successive days and had read the sermon to his father more than once. His father, moreover, had been looking forward to this hour with the greatest pleasure and anticipation, and his mother had been anxious lest he should be assailed by the evil eye. Indeed he had hardly gone out that day to go to the mosque ere she got some live coals, put them in a vessel and began to throw on top various kinds of incense. Then she proceeded to go round the house from room to room and to stay in each room some minutes, murmuring incantations the while. This she did until her son came home and then she met him from behind the door breathing forth incense and incantations. Meanwhile the sheikh was very angry cursing this man who had been consumed with envy to such an extent that he had debarred his son from preaching and leading the people in prayer.

There was another learned sheikh in the town who belonged to the Shafi'y rite. He was Imam of the mosque and the one who preached and led the prayers. He was well known for his piety and godliness and people went to such lengths of admiration and glorification as almost to canonise him.

They used to ask his blessing, and had recourse to him for the curing of their sick and to fulfil their needs, as though he perceived in himself some saintly power.

Even years after his death people continued to speak well of him and related with conviction, how, when he was being lowered into his tomb, he cried in a voice that all the mourners heard, 'Oh God, make it a blessed mansion!' They also used to relate how in their dreams they had seen that this man had received a good reward from God and what favours were prepared for him in Paradise.

There was a third sheikh in the city who belonged to the Maliky sect, but he did not devote himself to learning, nor did he take it as a vocation. He tilled the soil and engaged in trade and merely went to the mosque regularly to perform the five daily prayers. He would sit with people from time to time, reciting tradition to them and giving them religious instruction humbly and without boasting or bragging. But except for a few, they did not pay any attention to him.

These then were the ulema, but there were other learned scattered throughout the town and the neighbouring villages and countryside, who were no less influential than the official ulema with the mass of the people; nor had they less authority over their minds.

Among these was a certain pilgrim,[23] a tailor whose shop almost faced the village school. The general opinion about him was that he was miserly and mean.

He was connected with one of the great sheikhs of the Sufis and despised the whole company of the ulema because they derived their learning from books and not from sheikhs, for in his opinion the only real learning was the Divine Learning which descends upon the heart from God himself, without resorting to a book, and without having even to read or write.

There was also a certain sheikh who had commenced life as a donkey-boy carrying people's goods and chattels from place to place. Then he became a merchant and his donkeys were confined to the carrying of his own merchandise.

The general opinion about him was also that he had devoured

the wealth of orphans and had become rich at the expense of the weak.

He used to repeat and interpret the following verse times without number, 'Lo! Those who devour the wealth of orphans wrongfully, they do but swallow fire into their bellies, and they will be exposed to a burning flame.'

He disliked praying in the chief mosque because he hated the Imam and others of the ulema, and so he used to prefer to pray in a small unpretentious mosque of no importance.

There was yet another sheikh who could neither read nor write, nor even say the Fatiha properly. But he was a Shazly, that is to say a leader of one of the Sufi sects. He used to gather people together for the Zikr, and also give rulings on their spiritual and wordly affairs for them.

In addition to them there were the fuqaha who used to recite the Quran and to teach people to recite it. They were distinguished from the ulema by being called 'Bearers of the Book of God', and came in contact with the common people and women in particular. The majority of them were blind. They used to visit houses and recite the Quran and the women used to converse with them, asking for their rulings in matters of prayer and fasting, not to mention other affairs of theirs.

Now these fuqaha had a learning entirely different from that of the ulema, who derived their learning from books and had some sort of connection, however small, with Al-Azhar. Their learning was also different from that of the Sufis.

The people of divine inspiration used to derive their learning directly from the Quran. They interpreted it as best they were able, neither literally nor in the way in which it ought to be interpreted.

Indeed they interpreted it just as 'Our Master' did (and he was the brightest of the fuqaha, the strongest in learning and the most able at interpretation). The lad said to him one day, 'What is the meaning of the Word of God: "Khalaqna-kum atwaran"[24] – "We have created you in stages"?' He replied quietly and confidently, 'We have created you like oxen so that you do not understand anything.'

Or they interpreted the Quran as the lad's own grandfather, who knew the Quran by heart better than most people and was quicker than most at understanding, explanation and interpretation. One day his grandson asked him the meaning of a verse the interpretation of which is as follows: 'And among mankind is he who worshippeth Allah upon a narrow marge so that if good befalleth him he is content therewith but if trial befalleth him, he falleth away utterly. He loseth both the world and the thereafter.' He replied: 'Harf (marge) means on the edge of a sofa or a stone bench ... so that if good comes his way he sits back securely in his place, but if evil befalls him he tumbles forward on his face.'

Our lad used to mix freely with all these ulema and took something from them all, so that he gathered together a vast amount of assorted knowledge which was confused and contradictory. I can only reckon that it made no small contribution to the formation of his mind, which was not free from confusion, conflicting opinions and contradictions.

Fifteen

Sheikhs of the Sufis – What might they be? They were many in number and scattered throughout the regions of the land. The town was scarcely ever free from them. Their sects were different and they split up the people between them into schisms and divided their affections to a very great degree. There was acute rivalry in the province between two families of the Sufis; one held sway in the upper part of the province and the other in the lower part.

However, since the people of the province move about and think nothing of migrating from village to village or from town to town within the province, it happened that the followers of one family would settle in a district where the other family held sway.

Now the leaders of the two families used to move about the province visiting their followers and adherents. And Ye Gods! what animosities were aroused when the chief of the upper region came down to the lower or the chief of the lower region visited the upper.

The lad's father was a follower of the chief of the upper region and had taken the oath of allegiance to him, as his father had done before him. The lad's mother was also a follower of the chief of the upper region; in fact her father had been one of his assistants and intimate disciples. The chief of the upper region had died and had been succeeded by his son, the pilgrim. . . . This man was more active than his father and had a greater capacity for trickery, rapacity and arousing animosities. Moreover he was nearer to worldly things than his father and farther removed from the things of religion.

The lad's father had gone down to the lower part of the province and had settled there, and it was the custom of the chief of the upper part to visit him once every year. When he came he did not come alone or with a few people but with a mighty army, the number of which, if it did not reach a hundred, fell not far short of it. He did not take the train or any Nile boats, but instead he proceeded on his way, surrounded by his companions mounted on horses, mules and asses. As they passed through villages and small towns they alighted and mounted in strength and magnificence, victorious in a place where they alone held sway, and united in a place where their opponents were at all powerful.

Thus they came when they visited the lad's family, and when they arrived the street was filled with them and their horses, mules and asses.

They occupied it from the canal to its southern extremity. Ere long a lamb was killed and tables laid out in the street, and soon they fell upon their food with a gluttony that was almost unbelievable.

Meanwhile the sheikh was sitting in the guest-room, surrounded by his chosen friends and devotees, and the owner of the house and his household were in front of him carrying out his behests. When they had finished their lunch they went away and left him to sleep where he was. Later he got up and wished to perform the ceremonial ablutions (before prayer). Then see how the people vie with one another and quarrel as to who shall pour the water on him! And when that is done see how they race and quarrel to get a drink of the water of his ablutions! But the sheikh was too preoccupied to heed them. He prayed and made supplications at great length.

When at last he had finished all this he gave an audience to the people and they flocked to him, some kissing his hand and going away meekly, some holding conversation with him for a moment or so, and others asking him about some affair, and the sheikh would answer them with strange, vague expressions that they could interpret pretty much as they liked.

The lad was brought to him and he touched his head, quoting a verse from the Quran: 'And he taught you what you knew not, and the grace of God was mighty upon you.' From that day the lad's father was convinced that his son was destined to become great.

After the sunset prayer the tables were laid again and they ate. Then followed the evening prayer and then the assembly was held. The holding of the assembly means that people congregate at a dervish circle for Zikr. They start the Zikr sitting in silence. Then they begin to move their heads and raise their voices a little. Then a shudder runs through their bodies and lo! they are all standing, having leapt up into the air like jacks-in-the-boxes. The sheikhs move about the circle, reciting the poetry of Ibn Farid and similar poems.[25]

Now this sheikh was particularly fond of a well-known ode in which there is mention of the Prophet's Night Journey and Ascent. It begins as follows:

'From Mecca and the Most Glorious House
To Jerusalem travelled by night Ahmad'.

The sheikhs used to chant this continually and the performers of the Zikr used to move their bodies in time to this chant, bending and straightening themselves as though these sheikhs were making them dance.

Whatever the lad forgets he will never forget the night on which one of the reciters made a mistake and interpolated a phrase in the place of a phrase of the ode. Forthwith the sheikh got excited and boiled and foamed and frothed, crying at the top of his voice, 'You sons of bitches, may God curse your fathers, and your fathers' fathers, and your fathers' fathers' fathers as far as Adam! Do you want to bring destruction on this man's house?'

And whatever the lad forgets he will never forget the effect of this outburst of wrath upon the hearts of the performers of the Zikr and the other people present. It was just as though the people were convinced that the mistake in this ode was a source of bad luck without parallel.

The lad's father at first showed agitation and consternation, but later appeared more confident and tranquil. When on the morrow, after the sheikh had taken his departure, the family talked about him and what had taken place between him and the performers and reciters of the Zikr, the owner of the house laughed in a way such as left no doubt in the lad's mind afterwards that the faith of his father in this sheikh was not free from doubt and contempt. ... Yes, doubt and contempt! Certainly the greediness and covetousness of the sheikh were too obvious for anybody with the slightest degree of discrimination or reflection to be taken in.

The person who loathed the sheikh most and was most indignant about him was the lad's mother. She hated his visit and found his presence unbearable. She performed what she performed, and prepared what she prepared with hatred and indignation, so much so that she managed to bridle her tongue only with the greatest difficulty. The reason was that the visit of the sheikh was a heavy burden on this family, which, although it lived comfortably, was on the whole poor.

The visit of the sheikh consumed a great deal of wheat, cooking fat, honey, and things like that. Moreover it put the owner of the house to the trouble of borrowing in order to buy what was necessary in the way of lambs and goats. For the sheikh never descended upon this family without staying until the following day; and when he took his departure he also took with him anything that took his fancy and pleased him. At one time he would take a carpet, at another a Kashmir shawl; and so on.

Yet the visit of him and his companions was something which

the family heartily desired because it enabled them to boast, hold up their heads and outdo their neighbours. But still they hated it because it cost them what it did in the way of money and trouble.

In fact it was an ineluctable evil, established by custom and meeting the desire of the people.

Now the connection of the family with one of the Sufi sects was strong and lasting. It left among them many lasting traces in the way of information, stories and talk about miracles and supernatural events.

Both parents of the lad took great delight in relating all this information and talk to their children, and his mother never missed an opportunity of telling the following story:

'My father, together with my grandmother, once made the pilgrimage with Sheikh Khalid. Now the sheikh had made the pilgrimage three times, my father accompanying him on each occasion. This time his mother came too.

'Now when they had accomplished the pilgrimage and had gone on to Medina, the old lady fell from her camel-saddle into the road, and her back was badly broken, so that she was completely unable to walk or move at all. Her son began to carry her from place to place himself, but he found this so irksome and troublesome that he complained to the sheikh one day.

'The sheikh said to him, "Didn't you aver that she was a sherifa (descendant of the prophet) from the line of Hassan son of Aly?" "Yes," he replied, "that is so." "Then," said the sheikh, "she is going to her grandfather. When you have brought her to the Mosque of the Prophet, put her down at one side of it and leave her there with her grandfather to do with her as he wishes."

'So the man did so. He put his mother down in one of the corners of the mosque, and addressing her in the harsh language of the fellah, which notwithstanding its roughness is filled with love and tenderness, said, "There you are with your grandfather. I have no concern with either of you." Then he left her and followed the sheikh, as they wished to walk round the tomb of the Prophet. To quote the man's own story: "By God, I had only gone a few paces when I heard my mother calling me. When I looked round, she was standing up and walking and when I refused to return to her, she actually ran after me, and having overtaken me and got to the sheikh first, proceeded to walk round the tomb with the others".'

The lad's father never missed an opportunity of telling the following tale about the sheikh: 'Someone said in his presence that according to Al-Ghazzaly in one of his books,[26] the Prophet could not be seen in a dream. Then the sheikh was angry and said, "I thought better of you, O Ghazzaly! I have seen him with my own eyes riding his she-mule." And when that was mentioned to him on another occasion, he said, "I thought better of you, O Ghazzaly! I have seen him with my own eyes riding his she-camel".'

From this the lad's father concluded that Al-Ghazzaly had made a mistake, and that the generality of mankind were able to see the Prophet in dreams; and that saints and pious folk were able to see him, even when they were awake. The lad's father used to base this on a tradition, which he used to quote whenever he related this story. It is as follows: 'Whoso sees me in a dream has seen me as I really am, for Satan does not impersonate me'.

In this fashion the lad learnt all kinds of information about wonders and miracles, as well as Sufi mysteries.

And so it was that, whenever he wished to talk about anything like that to his companions and fellows at the school, they would relate similar tales to him, which they attributed to the chief of the lower region and in which they believed implicitly.

The country people, including their old men, youths, lads and women, have a particular mentality in which is simplicity, mysticism and ignorance. And those who have had the greatest share in producing this mentality are the Sufis.

Sixteen

It was not long ere our lad added another kind of knowledge to that which he had already acquired, and that was the science of magic and spells.

Now book-pedlars used to travel about among the villages and towns with an assortment of tomes, which perhaps furnishes the truest example of the mentality of the country people at that time.

They used to carry in their bags 'The Virtues of the Pious' and tales of the conquests and raids,[27] the story of the Cat and the Mouse and the debate between the wire and the engine, the Big Sun of Education in Magic, and another of which I don't remember the exact title, except that it was called the Diarby book.

Then there were various collects, stories of the Prophet's birth, collections of Sufi poetry, books of sermons and spiritual guidance, others of discourses and wonderful information: then again tales of the heroes of the Hilalites and Zanatites, and Antarah and Zahir Baibars and Saif Ibn Zy Yazan, and, together with all this, the Holy Quran.

People used to buy all these books, and devour their contents greedily, and so their minds are composed of the substance of it, just as their bodies are made up of the digest of what they eat and drink.

Our friend had had all this read to him and he had learnt by heart a considerable amount of it. But he concerned himself with two things in particular, and they were Magic and Sufism. There was nothing incongruous in the association of these two kinds of learning, nor was it difficult, since the contradiction which appears between them is really only on the surface. Does not the Sufi assure himself and other people that he can penetrate the veil of the unknown, tell what happened in the past, and foretell the future, as well as overstep the limits of natural laws? Moreover, he produces many kinds of supernatural wonders and miracles.

And what is the magician? Does he not assure himself of his power to obtain information about the unknown, and does he not exceed the limits of natural laws also? Does he not also claim connection with the world of spirits? ... Yes. ... The only difference you will find between a magician and a Sufi is that the latter is on the side of the angels and the former on the side of the devils. However, in order to arrive at something like a true understanding of their difference, we must read Ibn Khaldun and others like him, and deduce therefrom the scientific bases for the rejection of magic and the avoidance of it, and the appreciation of Sufism and the encouragement of a desire for it.

But nothing could be further from the minds of our lad and his companions than Ibn Khaldun and his like.[28] The only works that fell into their hands were books of magic, the virtues of the pious, and the miracles of the saints. These they read and were duly impressed. Then it was not long before they passed from reading and admiration to imitation and experiment. And so they followed out the Sufi practices and produced all kinds of magic arts.

Not infrequently did they confuse in their minds magic and Sufism, so that these two became one thing, and its aim, prosperity in life and propinquity to God.

So it was in the heart of our friend. He would be a Sufi and practise magic, all the while believing that he was pleasing God and getting out of life the best of its pleasures.

Among the stories brought by the book-pedlars, which were often in the hands of the lads, was one which was an excerpt from *The Arabian Nights*, and known as the story of Hassan of Basra.[29] This story contained an account of the adventures of a Magician who turned brass into gold, and also an account of that castle which stood behind the mountain on lofty pillars in the air, wherein resided the seven daughters of the Jinn, and whither Hassan of Basra repaired. Then again came the adventures of this man Hassan, telling how he made a long and difficult journey to the abodes of the Jinn. Now among these adventures there was something that filled the lad with admiration, and that was the account of the rod given to this Hassan on one of his journeys, one of the special properties of which was that, if you struck the ground with it, the earth split open and there came forth nine persons to carry out the behests of the possessor of the rod. They were of course Jinn, all-powerful and ethereal, who flew, ran, carried heavy burdens, removed mountains and worked wonders without limit.

The lad was fascinated by this wand, and so greatly desired to get possession of it that he was sleepless at night and perturbed by day. So he began to read books on magic and Sufism and sought among magicians and Sufis for a means of getting hold of it.

Now he had a relative, a lad like himself, who accompanied him to the village school, and who was even keener on the wand than he was himself. So what did they do but concentrate all their efforts on an investigation, so that they might arrive at some method which would enable them to get what they both so desired.

They eventually found it in the book of Diarby, and the process was as follows: After purification the man must retire apart by himself and put in front of him a brazier and a quantity of incense. Then he must begin to repeat the following name of God, 'Ya Latif! Ya Latif!' (O Kind One!), throwing some of the incense into the fire from time to time. He must continue repeating this word and burning this incense until the earth turns him round and the wall is cleft before him, and the servant of the Jinn appears who is answerable to this particular name of God. Then he may ask for what he wants and the behest will be indubitably obeyed.

The two lads had no sooner got hold of this formula than they determined to make use of it. They bought all manner of incense, and our lad drew apart by himself to the guest-room, closed its door on himself, and, putting in front of him some live coals, he began to throw incense into it, and to repeat, 'Ya Latif! Ya Latif!' He continued to do this for a long time, expecting the earth to spin around him, the wall to be cleft and the servant of the Jinn to appear before him, but nothing at all like that happened. At this point our lad was changed from a Sufi magician into a trickster.

He rushed out of the room excitedly holding his head with both hands while his tongue could hardly utter a word. His friend, the other lad, met him and asked him if he had encountered the servant and had asked him for the wand. But our friend could only reply excitedly and tremblingly, and his teeth chattered so much that he terrified his companion. After much trouble he began to calm down and to reply in disjointed phrases and in a hushed voice, 'The ground revolved about me, so that I nearly fell down, the wall split open and I heard a voice which filled every corner of the room. After that I fainted and as soon as I came to, I rushed out with all speed!'

The other lad listened to all this and was filled with joy and admiration of his friend. 'Take it easy,' he said, 'you were overcome with fright, and fear got the better of you. Let us search in the book for something that will reassure you and encourage you to be steadfast in the face of the servant, and ask him for what you want.'

Their investigation led them to discover that the one who retires must pray two rak'as (prostrations in prayer) before seating himself before the fire and chanting 'Ya Latif!'

So the lad did this on the morrow and began throwing incense into the fire and repeating the prayer of the Kind One in the expectation of the earth turning about him, the wall being cleft for him and the servant appearing before him, but nothing of the kind happened.

Then the lad went out to his friend calmly and confidently and told him that the earth had revolved about him, that the wall had split open and that the servant had appeared before him and had listened to his request, but was unwilling to grant it until he had practised solitude, and had prayed, burnt incense and made mention of God a number of times. Moreover before granting his request he had stipulated that a period of a whole month must elapse during which he should carry out this programme regularly, and if there was any break in the regularity of it, he must begin again and carry it out for another whole month.

The other lad believed his friend implicitly and began to urge him to seclude himself every day with the fire and to repeat the prayer, so the lad began to exploit this weakness on the part of his friend, and used to put him to any amount of hardship and trouble, and, if he refused or showed any signs of refusing, our friend would notify him that he would neither seclude himself with the fire nor say the prayer of Al-Latif nor ask for the wand, and then he would promptly submit.

However, our friend did not incline towards magic and Sufism of his own accord, but rather was driven to it, and the one who drove him was his father.

That was because the sheikh needed many things from God. He also had many sons and was keen on bringing them up and educating them, but he was so poor that he could not afford to pay for their education. And so he used to borrow from time to time and the payment of the debt was a burden to him. Wherefore he was desirous that his pay might be increased at intervals, or that he might be promoted to a higher class, or that he might be transferred from one employment to another, and he used to ask all this from God by means of prayers, supplication and divination.

Now his favourite mode of entreaty was the repetition of 'Ya Sin'.[30] He used to ask his son, the lad, to do this, because in the first place he was a lad and secondly he was blind, and by reason of these two merits he was preferred in the sight of God and ranked high in His estimation.

How could God be pleased to turn a deaf ear to a blind lad when he asked Him for anything, entreating Him by reciting the Quran?

This repetition of 'Ya Sin' was in three grades. In the first grade the suppliant withdraws apart by himself and recites this chapter of the Quran four times, then he asks for what he wants and goes away.

In the second grade the man withdraws apart by himself, recites this sura seven times, then asks for what he wants and goes away.

In the third grade the man withdraws apart by himself and recites this sura forty-one times, and every time he finishes it, he says the prayer of 'Ya Sin' after it. 'O company of the best among the best of peoples', and when the recitation is finished he asks for what he wants and goes away. Incense is obligatory in the third stage.

Now for small matters the sheikh used to require him to perform the shortest repetition, and for more important affairs the one of medium length; and for things which concerned the life of the family as a whole, the longest one.

So that if he was trying to get one of his sons into a school without payment, it would be the shortest repetition; if he wanted to beseech God to pay off a pressing debt, it would be the medium one; and if he wished to be transferred from one employment to another and his wages to be increased by a pound or part thereof, then it would be the longest one.

Every repetition had its price: the fee of the shortest repetition was a piece of sugar or sweetmeat, that of the medium one five milliemes, and that of the longest ten. Many a time did the lad retire and recite the chapter of 'Ya Sin' four or seven or forty-one times.

The strangest thing was that the requests were always granted, so that the sheikh's conviction that his son was blessed and superior in the sight of God was complete.

Magic and Sufism had other uses besides the granting of needs and prophecies of what the unknown would be. They surpassed this even to the extent of warding off evils and averting disasters.

The lad has forgotten many things, but he has not forgotten the alarm which filled the hearts of all the people in the town and the villages round about, when the news reached them from Cairo that a star with a tail would appear in the sky in a few days. Moreover at two o'clock in the afternoon it would touch the earth with the end of its tail and lo! it would become as chaff which is blown about by the winds.

However, the women and common people paid little or no attention to it. They only felt some alarm whenever they spoke about this disaster or heard the men talk about it, but ere long they went away and gave their thoughts to the practical affairs of life.

However, those versed in religious jurisprudence, the bearers of the Quran, the Sufis and their disciples were thoroughly anxious and alarmed, so that their hearts nearly burst from their sides and they argued about it incessantly.

Some said that the calamity would never come to pass, because it was contrary to what was known of the conditions of the Last Hour. For the world should not perish before 'The Beast, the Fire and the Anti-Christ' should appear, and before Christ should come down to the earth and fill it with justice, after it had been filled with oppression.

There were others who thought that this calamity was one of the conditions of the Last Hour; and yet others said that the calamity might happen in order that some sort of partial destruction should come upon the earth without destroying it in its entirety.

They used to argue about it all day long, and when night came and sunset prayers were over, they met together in circles in the mosque and in front of houses, and began to repeat this sentence: 'The Day of Wrath is nigh and God alone can dispel it' until the time of evening prayer.

The days passed and the appointed day came, but no star with a tail appeared in the sky nor did any sort of disaster, either great or small, overtake the earth.

Then those versed in religious jurisprudence, the bearers of the Quran and the Sufis were divided.

As for the people of learning, who derived their knowledge from books and who belonged to Al-Azhar, they triumphed. 'For,' they said, 'did we not tell you that this calamity could not happen before the conditions of the Last Hour? And did we not exhort you to disbelieve the astrologers?' But the bearers of the Quran said, 'No, the calamity nearly happened and would have done had not God shown kindness towards those giving suck, and those with child and the animals. Also he heard the prayers of those who prayed, and the supplication of the suppliants.'

And the Sufis and people of divine learning said, 'No, the calamity nearly happened, and would have done, but for the mediation of the Qutb-al-Mutawally[31] between the people and God. He averted this disaster from the people and he (the Qutb) bore their sins for them.'

You might say that the motive that moved people to fortify themselves against the Khamsin (winds) was that of magic and Sufism, but I can only tell you what the lad remembers of the days which preceded Sham-al-Nasim (Shem-el-Nessim).[32]

They were strange days, in which the hearts of women, lads and bearers of the Quran contained a mixture of joy and fear. On the Friday before, they would stuff themselves with special kinds of food and on the Saturday they would eat a surfeit of coloured eggs.

The fuqaha made great preparations for this day and having bought sheets of smooth white paper, they cut them up into very small thin pieces, and wrote on each piece 'Alif Lam Mim Sad' (A L M S).[33]

Then they folded these pieces up and filled their pockets with them. On Saturday they would visit the dwellings with which they had any connection and distribute these pieces of paper to their occupants, asking each person to swallow four pieces before touching food or drink. They assured the people that the swallowing of these pieces of paper would ward off from them the evils which the Khamsin winds brought, and particularly ophthalmia.

People believed them and swallowed these pieces of paper, paying the fuqaha for them with red and yellow eggs. The lad does not know what 'Our Master' did with all the eggs he collected on the Saturday of Light (Saturday before Easter). Often there were hundreds of them.

However, the preparation of the fuqaha for this day did not stop at the preparation of these pieces of paper. They used also to buy glossy white paper and cut it into long and rather wide strips, on which they wrote the relics of the Prophet: 'The relic(s) of Taha (the Prophet) were two rosaries, a copy of the Quran, a kohl case, two prayer mats, a millstone and a staff'.

And when they had finished this list of relics, they added to it a prayer, which began with the following words, which the fuqaha said were Syriac:

'Danbad danby, cary carandy, sary sarandy sabr, sabr batuna. (Imprison that which is far off lest it come to us, and that which is near lest it injure us) . . .'

Then they folded these strips of paper as charms and amulets and distributed them to the women and lads in the houses, taking in payment of them money, bread, pastry and various kinds of sweetmeats.

They assured people that by taking these charms and amulets they would protect themselves from those devils which the Khamsin winds brought. The women used to receive these charms and put great confidence in them, but that did not prevent them from taking precautions against the evil sprites ('afarit) on Sham-al-Nasim by splitting onions and hanging them on the doors of their homes; and also eating sprouting beans instead of any other food on that day.

Seventeen

It seemed that God wished to humiliate 'Our Master' through his pupil in no small degree.

Those incidents which took place from time to time, when the sheikh examined the lad, were not enough for him, nor the successive calamities which arose from the lad's keenness on learning the Alfiyya and other texts, which made the lad troublesome and rude, so that he exalted himself above his fellows and his master, imagining for himself a place among the ulema and disobeying the orders of the 'Arif.

No, all this was not enough, but there must fall another calamity, such as the man had never anticipated; a calamity far worse for him than the others, because it affected him in his work.

A man from Cairo came to the village in the capacity of inspector of agricultural roads. He was middle-aged, wore a tarbush, spoke French and gave out that he was a graduate of the School of Arts and Crafts.

He was a pleasant, likeable man and it was not long before people got to like him and to invite him to their houses and meetings, nor was it long ere bonds of friendship were established between him and the lad's father.

He commissioned 'Our Master' to read a sura of the Quran in his house every day, paying him ten piastres a month, which was a price such as only notables paid. Wherefore 'Our Master' liked this man and sang his praises.

However, Ramadan drew near, and the people used to meet on Ramadan night in the house of a certain notable of the town, who was a merchant, and 'Our Master' used to read the Quran at this man's house (every night) during the month.

The lad used to accompany 'Our Master' and relieve him from time to time by reciting a sura or part of one in his place.

One night, when he was reciting, the Inspector heard him, and said to his father, 'Your son is very weak at intoning the Quran.' The sheikh replied, 'He will improve his intonation, when he goes to Cairo, with one of the sheikhs of Al-Azhar.'

'I can teach him the intonation of the Quran, according to the reading of Hafs,'[34] said the Inspector, 'so that when he goes to Al-Azhar, he will have become acquainted with the foundations of intonation and it will be easy for him to devote himself to the seven, ten or fourteen readings.' 'Are you a bearer of the Quran?' asked the sheikh. 'Yes,' replied the Inspector, 'and I can also intone it. Moreover, if I were not busy, I would be able to make your son recite the Quran according to all the different versions. Nevertheless, I should like to devote an hour to him every day, in which I would make him recite the version of Hafs and teach him the elements of the art, thus giving him a sound preparation for Al-Azhar.'

The people began to say, 'How is it possible that one who wears a tarbush and speaks French should know the Quran and the versions of the different readings?'

'I am an Azharite,' said the Inspector. 'I reached an advanced stage in the study of religious sciences, then I left it for the schools, and eventually graduated from the School of Arts and Crafts.'

'Then recite something to us,' they cried. The man took off his shoes, crossed his legs and chanted to them the sura of Hud in a manner such as they had never heard.

Then you may imagine their admiration of him and the fuss they made of him; and you may imagine also how grieved and annoyed 'Our Master' was. The man spent the night like one who had been struck by lightning.

In the morning the sheikh ordered his son to go to the house of the Inspector every day. This greatly pleased the lad; he told companions at the school, and talked about it with the other lads.

You may imagine the grief that all this talk brought to the heart of 'Our Master'. So much so, that he reprimanded the lad and ordered him never to mention the name of the Inspector again in the school.

The lad went to the Inspector's house, and went there regularly.

The Inspector read with him a book called *Tuhfat-al-Atfal* (Children's Precious Gift), and explained to him the elements of intonation. He taught him 'Madd' (Prolongation of the voice on a vowel), 'Ghann' (Nasalisation), 'Ikhfa' (Lowering the voice), 'Idgham' (contraction of two letters into one), and all the things connected with these.

The lad was delighted with this learning, and used to talk about it to his companions at the school, explaining to them that 'Our Master' was no good at 'Madd' or 'Ghann', and knew neither the difference between 'Word and letter prolongation', nor the difference between 'Heavy prolongation' and 'Light prolongation'.

Echoes of all this reached 'Our Master' and caused him great grief and sorrow, till sometimes he was at his wits' end.

The lad began to go through the Quran with the Inspector from the beginning, and the Inspector taught him the proper punctuation.

The lad began to imitate the Inspector's chanting and copy his tune, reading the Quran after this fashion in the school. His father started to examine him and when he heard this new style of reading he was full of admiration and pleasure and praised the Inspector. Nothing annoyed 'Our Master' more than did this praise.

For a whole year the lad continued to go to this house and recite the Quran to the Inspector until he was certain of the intonation according to the version of Hafs.

He was about to start on the version of Warsh,[35] when certain events took place and the lad went to Cairo.

The lad liked going to this house very much because he admired the Inspector and was anxious to perfect his knowledge of the Quran and its intonation; also inasmuch as he annoyed 'Our Master' and at the same time manifested his superiority over his fellows.

Thus it was for the first two months of the year, but after that there was something else that attracted him to the Inspector's house and made him love it ... the Inspector was middle-aged, about forty or a little over, and he had married a young lady who was not yet sixteen. He had no children, and there were no other occupants of the house except the young lady and her grandmother, who was over fifty. When the lad first began to frequent this house, he used to come and go without seeing anyone except the Inspector. But it was not long before the young lady began to talk to him and to ask him about himself, his mother, his brothers and his home.

At first the lad answered her shyly, and then freely and confidently, so that a simple affection grew up between them that was dear to his soul and held a delicious spot in his heart. It annoyed the older woman, but the Inspector was in complete ignorance of it.

The lad took to going to the Inspector's house an hour or so before the appointment in order that he might converse with the young lady. She used to wait for him expectantly and as soon as he came she would conduct him to her room and, when she had sat down herself and bade him sit down, they would begin to converse.

Ere long conversation gave place to play – only such play as young people indulge in, no more and no less, but it was delightful play.

The lad related all this to his mother, who laughed and pitied the young lady, saying to his sister, 'Fancy a child married to this elderly man. She knows nobody and nobody knows her, so that she is in a bad way and in need of amusement and diversion.'

From that day the lad's mother tried to get to know the young lady and invited her to the house, telling her to come as often as she liked.

Eighteen

Thus the lad spent his days between the house, the village school, the law courts, the mosque, the Inspector's house, the assemblies of the learned and the circles of the Sufis (zikr). His life was neither entirely sweet nor bitter; sometimes it was sweet and sometimes bitter. In the intervals between it was languid and uneventful.

Then the day came, whereon the lad really tasted pain, and thereafter knew that the pains he had suffered previously and on account of which he had hated life were nothing at all; he also realised that Time is able to pain people and afflict them and yet at the same time endear life to them and make its course run smooth for them.

The lad had a little sister, who was four years old and the youngest of the family. She was a light-hearted little thing with a bright, open face, and a chatterbox whose conversation was pleasing, and she was endowed with a strong imagination.

Moreover, she was the delight of the whole family, and spent hours on end all alone playing and amusing herself. She used to sit down in front of the wall and talk to it, just as her mother talked to a neighbour, and whatever game it was, she put her whole spirit into it and clothed it with personality.

Thus this toy was a woman and that one a man, or this one a young man and that a young lady. The child used to come and go among all these individuals and invent conversations between them so that at one time they would converse lightly and playfully, at another with anger and annoyance, and again they would talk quietly and calmly. The whole family used to take great delight in listening to these conversations, and in watching these various games without the child seeing, hearing or feeling that anyone was watching her.

And now preparations for the Big Feast, 'Id-ul-Adha[36] of one year, were at hand. The lad's mother began to prepare for the Feast, putting the house in order for it and making bread and all manner of pastry. His brothers also made ready for the Feast, the elder ones going to the tailor and to the shoemaker, while the younger ones enjoyed themselves amid this unusual hustle and bustle in the house.

Our lad regarded all this rather philosophically as was his custom, for he had no need to go to either the tailor or the shoemaker, nor did he derive any amusement from this unusual hustle and bustle. He just stayed alone by himself and lived in the world of imagination which he derived from stories and the various books which he used to read and read to excess.

The preliminaries of the Feast were at hand, and one morning the child was somewhat languid and out of sorts, but scarcely anyone paid any attention to it. Now the children in the villages and towns of the provinces are exposed to this kind of neglect, particularly if the family is numerous and the mistress of the house has much work to do. For the women of the villages and towns of the provinces have a criminal philosophy and a knowledge that is no less criminal. The child complains and the mother seldom takes any notice. ... For what child does not complain? It is only a matter of a day and a night and then it gets over it and recovers. And if its mother does take any notice, she either despises the doctor or else is ignorant of him. And so she relies upon this criminal knowledge of women and those like them.

In this way our lad lost his eyesight. Ophthalmia attacked him, but he was neglected for some days. Then the barber was called in, and he treated him in a way that resulted in the loss of his sight.

In the same way this child lost her life. She seemed indisposed, languid and feverish for a day and a day and a day. She was lying down on her bed in a corner of the house, and from time to time her mother or her sister would pay attention to her, putting before her some food – God knows whether it was good or bad for her. There is continual hustle and bustle throughout the house. In one part bread and pastry are being made, and in another the guest-room and reception-room are being cleaned. The lads are at their games and play; the youths are thinking about their clothes and shoes. The sheikh comes and goes, and spends the latter part of the day and the early part of the night sitting with his friends.

At last came the afternoon of the fourth day and all this stopped abruptly. It stopped and the lad's mother realised that a shadow hung over the house. There had never been a death in this house before, nor had this tender-hearted mother ever tasted real pain.

She was going about her work, when the little girl began to utter horrible cries. Her mother at once left everything and hastened to her. The cries continued and increased, so that the child's sisters also left everything and hastened to her. The crying continued louder than ever, and the child twisted and turned in her mother's arms. The sheikh, too, left his friends and hastened to her. The cries continued louder than ever, and the little girl quivered horribly, her face contorted and sweat streaming down it; then the lads and youths left what they were about, their games or conversation, and hastened to her, but the cries only increased in volume.

There was the whole family stunned and speechless, surrounding the little girl and not knowing what to do. So it went on for two hours. The sheikh had been seized by that weakness that takes hold of men on occasions like these.

He went away murmuring prayers and verses of the Quran, beseeching God to hear him. The youths and lads stole away somewhat downcast, scarcely able to forget what they had been doing, their conversation and games, and yet scarcely able to continue it.

They remained like that in the house perplexed, and their mother was sitting stunned, gazing at her daughter and giving her all manner of medicine to drink. I don't know what it was.

The crying was incessant and increasing while the trouble continued to get worse. I never thought that children who were only fours years old were endowed with strength like this.

Supper-time came and the table was laid. The lad's eldest sister laid it, and the sheikh and his sons came and sat down, but the cries of the little girl were as loud as ever, and no one stretched a hand for food. They dispersed one and all, and the table was cleared just as it had been laid, and the little girl cried and tossed, while her mother gazed at her and sometimes stretched out her hands to heaven. She had uncovered her head, which it was not her custom to do.

But the gates of heaven were shut that day and the irrevocable decree had gone forth, so the sheikh could recite the Quran and the mother make supplications as much as they liked.

The strange thing was that no one in all this company of people thought about the doctor. As the night advanced the cries of the little girl began to die down, her voice began to grow feebler and her tossing began to subside.

The wretched mother imagined that God had heard herself and her husband, and that the crisis was passing. And in fact the crisis had begun to pass. God had taken pity on this little girl, and the dying down of the voice and the abating of the tossing were two signs of this mercy.

The mother looked at her daughter and imagined she was going to sleep. Then she looked again and saw that the stillness was unbroken by any sound or movement; only a slight breath, a very light breath, came repeatedly from the slightly open lips. Then this breathing stopped, and the little girl had departed from this life. What was her complaint and how did this complaint cause her death? God alone knows.

At this point another cry was raised and continued with increasing volume. And at this point another trouble manifested itself and continued with increasing force. However, it was not the cries of the little girl nor her trouble, it was the crying of the mother when she saw death, and her trouble when she felt her loss.

The youths and lads fled to their mother, but the sheikh had got to her first. She was beside herself with grief and distraction, her tongue uttering disjointed phrases and her voice broken with sobs. She slapped her cheeks violently and incessantly, while her husband stood in front of her unable to utter a word, the tears streaming down; and the neighbours, both men and women, hearing these cries, hastened to them.

So the sheikh went out to the men to receive their condolences with patience and fortitude, and the youths and lads dispersed throughout the house. Some, whose hearts were hardened, slept, while others, whose hearts were softer, kept awake. But the mother, in the midst of her grief and distraction with her daughter in front of her stiff and cold, wails, scratches her face, and beats her breast.

All around, her daughters and female neighbours are doing the same thing, wailing, scratching their faces, and beating their breasts, and so the whole night is spent.

There was no more loathsome hour than that in which some people came and carried the little girl away to a place whence she would not return.

That day was 'Id-ul-Adha (the Big Feast). The house had been put in order for the Feast, and the victims had been prepared. What a day and what a victim ! What a terrible hour when the sheikh returned to his house at noon having buried his daughter in the ground!

From that day on the family was never free from bereavement. Only a few months later the sheikh lost his aged father, and scarcely another few months had passed when the lad's mother lost her worn-out mother. It was a continual succession of grief and one blow followed hard on another; some were stinging and some mild.

At length came a terrible day, the like of which the family had never known, and which stamped its life with a perpetual grief. It turned the hair of both parents white, and caused the mother to wear black till the end of her days, and to lose all taste for pleasure. She never laughed but she wept afterwards; she never went to sleep without shedding a few tears nor woke up without shedding a few more; she never tasted fruit without first giving some to the poor or to boys; she never smiled during a Feast, nor did she greet a day of pleasure except with reluctance.

This day was the 21st August of the year 1902. The summer of that year was terrible. An epidemic of cholera descended upon Egypt and attacked the population like wildfire. It destroyed towns and villages, and wiped out whole families. Meanwhile 'Our Master' waxed fat on amulets and writing lists of the relics of the Prophet.

The village schools and town schools were closed and doctors and envoys of the Public Health Department were scattered throughout the land with their instruments and tents in which to isolate the sick.

Souls were filled with anxiety and hearts with fear. Life became a thing of no account for people. Every family talked about what had befallen the other and waited for their own share of disaster.

The lad's mother was in a perpetual state of anxiety, asking herself a thousand times a day on which of her sons or daughters the calamity would fall. Now she had a son eighteen years of age, who was good-looking and of pleasing appearance, a fine intelligent fellow.

In fact he was the best of the family, the most intelligent, the most tender-hearted, the best natured; the most dutiful and considerate to his father and mother and the most companionable to his little brothers and sisters.

Moreover he was always happy. He had taken the Baccalaureat certificate,[37] and his name was down for the School of Medicine. He was waiting for the end of the summer, when he would go to Cairo. When the epidemic broke out, he attached himself to the doctor of the town, and took to accompanying him on his rounds, saying that it would be practice for his future profession.

At last came the 21st August. The young man returned as usual smiling. He spoke kindly to his mother, joked with her and allayed her fears, saying, 'There were no more than twenty cases in the town to-day and the force of the epidemic has begun to abate.' But in spite of that he complained of some sickness, and went out to his father and sat down and talked to him, as was his custom. Later he went to his friends and accompanied them to a place where he went with them every day on the banks of the Ibrahimiyyah Canal.

In the early part of the night, he returned home and spent an hour laughing and playing with his brothers. That very night he told everyone in the house that eating garlic was a precaution against cholera. He ate it himself, and his brothers, big and little, followed his example. He tried to convince his parents of its efficacy but did not succeed.

At midnight the whole house was quiet and the occupants and animals alike were deep in slumber. Suddenly a strange cry rang through the still air and woke everybody up. Then the sheikh and his wife went to the long corridor, open to the sky, calling their son by name. The youths of the house leapt from their beds and hastened in the direction of the voice, while the lads sat up and rubbed their eyes, rather anxiously trying to make out whence this sound came and what this strange movement meant.

The source of all this was the sound of the young man trying to vomit. He had spent an hour or two there, having left his room on the tips of his toes, and having gone out into the open air to be sick, making every effort not to wake anyone up. At last the illness reached such a pitch that he could neither control himself nor vomit quietly, and his parents heard the retching and were alarmed by it, as were the other occupants of the house.

So the youth was stricken down, the plague had found its way into the house, and the young man's mother knew on which of her sons the calamity would fall.

That night the sheikh was truly worthy of admiration. He was calm and serene, although frightened, and controlled himself well. There was something in his voice that showed that his heart was broken and that in spite of this he was patiently prepared to bear the calamity. He took his son to his room and gave orders for his isolation from his brothers. Then he went out and called two of his neighbours and it was hardly an hour before he returned with the doctor.

Meanwhile the youth's mother, terror-stricken as she was, was patiently and faithfully tending her son. Whenever the vomiting gave him a rest, she went out into the corridor, raised her hands and face to the sky and wore herself out in supplications and prayers until she heard the retching again. Then she hastened to her son, supporting him on her breast and taking his head between her hands. But all the while her tongue never ceased from prayer and supplication.

She was not able to keep the patient apart from his big and little brothers. They filled his room and stood round him speechless. He joked with his mother every time the vomiting gave him a rest, and played with his small brothers until the doctor came and prescribed various things and gave various orders, and then departed, saying that he would return in the morning.

The young man's mother stayed in her son's room and the sheikh sat near at hand, speechless. He neither prayed nor made supplication; nor did he answer any of those who spoke to him. At length morning came and the young man began to complain of pain in his legs. His sisters came and rubbed his legs for him, while he suffered, sometimes out loud and sometimes concealing his pain, the vomiting straining him, and at the same time rending the hearts of his parents.

The whole family spent such a morning as they had never

known the like. A dark, silent morning in which there was something alarming and terrifying.

There was a crowd of folk outside the house, who had come to comfort the sheikh, and inside was a crowd of women who had come to console the young man's mother, but the sheikh and his wife were too busy to pay any heed to any of them. The doctor kept coming every hour or so.

The young man had asked that a wire should be sent to his brother, the Azharite, who was in Cairo, and also to his uncle, who was in the upper part of the province. He kept asking for a watch from time to time and looking at it, as though he was impatient of the time and was afraid to die without seeing his brother the youth or his elderly uncle.

What a terrible hour it was, that third hour of Thursday the 21st August, 1902! The doctor left the room, having given up hope, and confided in two of the sheikh's best friends that the young man was at his last gasp.

The two men went into the room where the young man was lying with his mother beside him, and on that day for the first time in her life, she appeared in the presence of men.

The young man was writhing on the bed. He stood up, then threw himself down, then sat up, then asked for a watch, then tried to be sick.

His mother was speechless with fear and when the two men tried to console him, he replied, 'I am not better than the Prophet, and did not the Prophet die?' He called his father, wishing to console him, but the sheikh did not answer him. He stood up, then he sat down and alternately threw himself on and off the bed. As for our lad he sat alone in a corner of the room, silent, downcast, bewildered, with grief simply tearing at his heart.

At last the young man threw himself down on the bed and was unable to move. He just uttered groans which occasionally died down, and the sounds gradually died away.

The lad will forget all else before he forgets the last groan which the young man uttered, a thin, weak, long drawn-out groan. Then he was silent.

At this moment the young man's mother got up, her patience

exhausted and her endurance at an end. Hardly had she stood up before she fell down, or would have done, had not the two men supported her. Then she pulled herself together and went out of the room with downcast eyes, walking quietly until she got outside, and then she poured forth from her bosom a cry that the lad never recalls without his heart being rent by it.

The young man tossed about a little, and there passed through his body a quiver which was followed by the silence of death. The two men approached and prepared the body. They bound his head about with a napkin, threw a veil over his face and went out to the sheikh.

Then they remembered the lad alone in one of the corners of the room, and one of them returned and dragged him out, distracted as he was, taking him to a place among the people and throwing him down there anyhow.

But an hour or so later the young man was prepared for burial, and the men carried him out on their shoulders.

How cruel is Fate! They had scarcely reached the door, when his uncle, the sheikh, appeared, just too late to console his nephew, who had resisted the approach of death in the hope that he would come.

From that day deep grief settled on the household and all appearance of pleasure or rejoicing, no matter what the occasion, had to be avoided by all both old and young.

From that day the sheikh would never sit down to his lunch or his supper without recalling his son and weeping for an hour or so. And in front of him his wife joined in the weeping, while round about him his sons and daughters endeavoured to console their parents; and their efforts being of no avail, they would fall to weeping one and all.

From that day the family used to cross the Nile and visit the cemetery from time to time, although before that they used to find fault with those who visited the dead.

From that day our lad's outlook on life was completely changed.

He really knew God and was at great pains to draw near to Him by every possible means, from alms-giving to earnest prayer and the recitation of the Quran.

God knows that it was neither fear nor compassion nor fondness of life that drove him to it, but the fact that he knew that his brother the youth had been a student and had neglected the performance of his religious duties. Therefore the lad went through all these forms of worship, wishing to take away some of the sins of his brother.

His brother had been eighteen years old when he died, and the lad had heard from the sheikhs that prayer and fasting were obligatory for a man when he reached the age of fifteen. Therefore he reckoned to himself that his brother owed God three whole years' prayer and fasting, and imposed upon himself the obligation to pray the five daily prayers twice every day, once for himself and once for his brother; and also to fast two months in the year, a month for himself and a month for his brother. He vowed he would hide this from all his people, and establish a special covenant between himself and God. Moreover before taking his own portion of whatever food came into his hands he would give some to a poor man or an orphan.

God is witness that the lad kept the covenant for months and never changed this mode of life until he went to Al-Azhar.

From that day the lad knew what night vigils were, for many a time he would spend the dark hours of a whole night, either thinking about his brother or reciting Surat-al-Ikhlas (The Chapter of Sincerity) thousands of times, all of which he would dedicate to his brother. Or else he would compose verses, after the manner of the poetry which he used to read in story books, in which he would mention his grief and pain at the loss of his brother, taking great care never to conclude the poem without a blessing on the Prophet and dedicating the reward of this blessing to his brother.

Yes, from that day the lad experienced terrifying dreams, the illness of his brother being depicted for him every night. This condition of affairs went on for some years, and then as he grew older and Al-Azhar wrought its change on him, the illness of his brother began to come to his mind only occasionally, and so the youth became a man.

But however much he has changed through the various stages of life, he remains as he was as regards his loyalty to this brother.

He remembers him and sees him in his dreams once a week at the very least.

The brothers and sisters of the young man have long ceased to mourn him and his friends and contemporaries have forgotten him. Moreover the memory of him comes less frequently to his father the sheikh. Yet there are two people who always remember him and will always do so daily as night draws on: they are his mother and this lad.

Nineteen

'Well, this time you are going to Cairo with your brother to become a student, and to exert yourself in the pursuit of learning. I hope I may live to see your brother a judge and you one of the ulema of Al-Azhar, sitting against one of its pillars and surrounded by a wide and far-flung circle.'

The sheikh said this to his son at the end of one autumn day in the year 1902.

When the lad heard this he neither believed nor disbelieved it, but preferred to wait its confirmation or refutation during the next few days. For his father had often spoken to him like that, and his brother the Azharite had made similar promises.

Then, later, the Azharite had returned to Cairo and the lad had stayed in the town dividing his time between the house, the village school, the law courts and the assemblies of the sheikhs.

In truth he did not know why his father's promise that year turned out to be true, but he informed the lad one day that he would leave in a few days' time. Thursday came and the lad actually found himself preparing for the journey. He found himself at the station before sunset, sitting in a squatting position, with bowed head, downcast and sad. He heard his eldest brother rebuking him gently and saying, 'Do not hang your head like that, and put on that sad face, or you will make your brother unhappy.' And he heard his father encouraging him kindly and saying, 'Why are you sad? Are you not a man? Can you not be separated from your mother? Do you always want to be idle? Was not this long period of idleness sufficient for you?'

God knows that the lad was sad, not because he was to be separated from his mother or because he would never play again, but because he was thinking of the brother who slept over there beyond the Nile. He was thinking of him and remembering how often his dead brother used to reflect that he would be together with his two brothers in Cairo, when he became a student at the School of Medicine.

When he remembered this he was sad, but he said nothing, nor did he manifest his grief. He only pretended to smile, for if he had given way to his natural inclination he would have wept and caused those about him, his father and brothers, to weep.

The train started, the hours passed and our friend found himself in Cairo among a crowd of students who had come to meet his brother. They greeted him and ate the food he had brought for them. So the day ended.

It was Friday and the lad found himself at Al-Azhar for prayers. He listened to the preacher, a sheikh with a deep, loud voice, who rolled out his 'qafs' and 'rays' sonorously. Otherwise there was no difference between him and the preacher in his town. The sermon was the same one as he had been accustomed to hear at home. The tradition was the same. The second sermon was the same. The prayers were neither longer nor shorter than those he was accustomed to.

The lad returned to his house, or rather to his brother's room, somewhat disappointed. His brother said to him, 'What do you think of the rendering of the Quran and the study of the readings?' The lad replied, 'I am not in need of any of this, for I have perfected my rendering and I do not need the readings. Have you studied the readings yourself? Is it not sufficient that I should be like you? I am more in need of learning. I want to study jurisprudence (Fiqh), syntax (Nahu), logic (Mantiq) and the doctrine of the Unity (Tawhid).'

His brother replied, 'That will do for you! It will be sufficient for you to study jurisprudence (Fiqh) and syntax (Nahu) this year.'

Saturday came, and the lad got up at dawn, performed his ablutions and prayed. His brother in like manner arose, performed his ablutions and prayed. Then he said, 'You will come with me now to such and such a mosque, and attend a lecture that is not meant for you, but only for me, so that when it is over I can take you to Al-Azhar and find you a sheikh from among my friends to whom you can go and from whom you can learn the principles of learning.'

The lad said, 'What is this lecture which I shall attend?' His brother replied laughingly, 'It is a lecture on jurisprudence, and the book is that of Ibn 'Abidin on Al-Durr.'[38] He said all this rolling it on his tongue. 'Who is the sheikh?' asked the lad. 'He is Sheikh . . .' here the lad heard a name which he had heard a thousand and one times, for his father had mentioned the name and boasted that he had known him when he was a provincial judge. His mother had also mentioned this name, and recalled that she had known his wife as a tall, foolish, rustic wench, who imitated town fashions, when she had not at all the style of townspeople.

The lad's father used to ask his Azharite son about the sheikh every time he came back from Cairo, and about his lecture and the number of his students.

His son the Azharite used to tell him about the sheikh and his position at the High Court and his circle of students, which numbered hundreds.

The lad's father used to press his son the Azharite to read as the sheikh read. When the young man tried to imitate him, his father would laugh in pride and admiration.

The lad's father used to say to his son, 'Does the sheikh know you?' And the young man would answer. 'How should he not? I and my friends are his favourite pupils and enjoy his special favour. We attend the public lecture and then we attend a private lecture with him in his house. Very often we lunch with him so that we can work with him afterwards at one of the many books he is writing.'

Then the young man would go on to describe the sheikh's house, his reception room and library. His father would listen to all this with admiration, and when he went out to meet his friends, he would tell them what he had heard from his son with pride and vainglory.

The lad then knew of the sheikh, and was pleased at the prospect of going to his circle and hearing him. How happy he was when he put off his shoes at the door of the mosque and walked first on the straw-mat, then on the marble and then on the thin carpet, which was spread over the floor of the mosque! How happy he was when he took his place among the circle on this carpet by the side of a marble pillar. He touched the pillar and liked its glossy smoothness, pondering for a long time on his father's remark, 'I hope I may live to see your brother a judge and you lecturing by a pillar in Al-Azhar.'

While he was pondering thus and wishing to touch the pillars of Al-Azhar and to see if they were like the pillars of this mosque, a strange hum came from the students around him. Suddenly he felt the hum die down and then stop abruptly. His brother poked him with his finger, saying in an undertone, 'The sheikh has come.'

The lad's whole being was centred in his ears at that moment, and he listened. What did he hear? He heard a voice that was low, gentle and serene, filled with conceit or dignity – call it what you will. Anyhow it was strange, and the lad did not like it.

For some minutes the lad was unable to make out a word of what the sheikh was saying, until his ears became accustomed to the voice of the sheikh and the echoes of the place. Then he heard, interpreted and understood.

He swore to me afterwards that from that day he despised learning.

He heard the sheikh saying, 'If he says to her, "You are divorced, or you are bivorced, or you are debauched, or you are dehorsed, the divorce holds good, no matter how distorted the pronunciation is".'

This he said in a sing-song voice, composing a chant for it; a voice that was not entirely free from harshness although its owner tried to make it sweet.

Then he brought this song to a close with a phrase which he employed continually throughout his lecture, 'Fahim ya 'ad‘a?'[39]

The lad began to ask himself what this word "ad'a" was. At last, as they went out from the lecture, he asked his brother, 'What is 'ad'a?' His brother burst out laughing and said, "ad'a is a 'gad'a (fellow) in the language of the sheikh.'

After that he took him to Al-Azhar and introduced him to his tutor, who instructed him in the principles of jurisprudence (Fiqh) and syntax (Nahu) for a whole year.

Twenty

You, my little daughter, are innocent, uncorrupted and pure in heart. You are nine years old, and at this age children admire their fathers and mothers and make them their ideals in life, imitating them in word and deed and trying to be like them in everything; they boast about them when they talk to their companions during playtime, and it seems to them that they were in their childhood just as they are now, good examples and excellent models.

Is it not as I say? Do you not think that your father is the best and noblest of men? Do you not think also that he was the best and noblest of children? Are you not convinced that his mode of life was like yours or even better? Would you not like to live as your father lived when he was eight years old? In spite of that, your father has spent every effort he possesses and has gone to almost unendurable pains to spare you the life he had when he was a lad.

I knew him, my daughter, at this stage of his life. Moreover, if I were to tell you of his condition at that time, your dreams would be shattered and you would be very disappointed in your expectations. Besides, I should open in your innocent heart and sweet soul one of the floodgates of grief, which it would be a sin to open while you are at this delightful stage of your life. But I will not tell you anything about your father at that stage until you are a little older, and can read, understand and judge for yourself. Then you will be able to realise that your father really loved you and really did his best for your happiness, and that he was partially successful in sparing you his childhood and boyhood.

Yes, my daughter, I knew your father at this stage of his life. I am sure that in your heart there is mercy and tenderness, but I am equally afraid that, if I told you what I knew about your father, you would not be able to restrain your pity, and, being overcome with compassion, you would burst into tears.

I saw you one day sitting on your father's lap, while he told you the story of Œdipus Rex, how he went out of his palace when he had put out his eyes and did not know how to proceed. Then his daughter, Antigone, came and led him and guided him.

On that day I saw you listening to the story with pleasure at first. Then little by little you began to change colour and you gradually puckered up your smooth forehead; it was not long before you burst into tears and falling upon your father smothered him with kisses. Then your mother came and snatched you from his arms, staying with you until you were comforted.

Your father and mother, and I as well, understood that you only wept because you saw in Œdipus your blind father, who also can neither see nor find his way by himself. So you wept for your father just as much as you wept for Œdipus. I know very well, too, that you have in you the levity of children and their inclination to make fun of and laugh at things, together with their callousness. And I am afraid, my daughter, that if I were to tell you of your father's condition at some stages of his boyhood, you would laugh at him cruelly and callously. And I should not like a child to laugh at its father, neither should I like it to make fun of him nor to be hard on him.

However, I knew your father at one stage of his life, and I am able to tell you about it without plunging you into grief or tempting you to laugh or make fun of him.

I knew him at the age of thirteen, when he was sent to Cairo to take up his studies of learning at Al-Azhar, and at that time he was a hard-working, diligent lad. He was thin, pale, with a neglected appearance, and rather on the poor side. Indeed he was conspicuous in his dirty cloak, and his cap which had changed from white to black, and also in his shirt, which showed from under his cloak and which had become multi-coloured owing to the quantities of food that had been spilled down it, and a pair of worn-out and patched shoes.

He was conspicuous for all this, but nevertheless pleasing to the eye when its gaze fell on him, notwithstanding his ragged state and sightless eyes, with his untroubled brow and smiling mouth, hurrying with his guide to Al-Azhar. He stepped unfalteringly and did not hesitate in his walk, and there did not appear on his face that darkness which usually covers the faces of the blind.

He was conspicuous but pleasing to the eye, and he aroused some sympathy when its gaze fell on him in the lecture circle, as he listened intently to the sheikh and devoured his speech greedily, smiling without irritation or complaint. Moreover, he showed no inclination to play while the other lads played and fidgeted.

I knew him, my daughter, at this stage, and how I should like you to have known him as I knew him, for then you would appreciate what a difference there is between you. But how could this be for you, while you are only nine years old, and see life as rosy and pleasant?

I knew him when he spent days, weeks, months and years only eating one kind of food, of which he took his portion morning and evening, without complaining or grumbling. His was no patient endurance, for he did not think of his state as being worse than that of others.

If you, my daughter, were to take even a small portion of this dish one day, your mother would be so concerned about you that she would give you a dose of salts and be prepared to call in the doctor.

Your father spent weeks and months living on nothing but bread of Al-Azhar, and the Azharites were lucky if they did not find in it various kinds of straw and pebbles and all manner of insects.

For weeks and months he only dipped this bread in black treacle. You do not know what black treacle is, and it is a good thing for you that you do not.

Thus your father lived, working hard and facing life and his work with a smile. In want, yet scarcely feeling privation, until the year came to an end and he returned to his parents, who came to meet him and asked him how he ate and how he lived. Then he began to concoct lies for them, just as he is accustomed to make up stories for you, telling them that the life he led was all ease and pleasure.

It was not mere love of lying which led him to this mendacity, but only that he was sorry for these two old folk, and hated to tell them of the privation he had really endured. Moreover, he was also concerned for his brother, the Azharite, and did not want his parents to know that he took more than his share of the comforts of life.

Such was the life of your father, when he was thirteen years old.

Then you will ask me how he attained the position in which he is now. And how his appearance became presentable and no longer conspicuous and repulsive. And how he was able to give you and your brother the agreeable life you now enjoy. How has he been able to arouse in the hearts of many people what he has aroused, in the way of envy, hatred and malice? And how has he been able to arouse in the hearts of others the approval, respect and encouragement that he has? If you were to ask how he has passed from that state to this, I could not answer you.

But there is somebody else who is able to give the answer, and who may tell you if you ask. Do you know who it is? Look! It is the Guardian Angel, who bends over your bed when evening comes that you may greet the night in tranquillity and in sweet sleep, and who bends over your bed when morning comes that you may greet the day in pleasure and happiness.

Surely you are indebted to this Angel for the tranquillity of night and the pleasure of day, which you enjoy. This Angel, my little girl, has watched over your father and has brought him happiness in the place of misery, and hope out of despair; out of poverty wealth, and out of trouble joy and felicity.

The debt of your father to this Angel is no less than yours, so try to co-operate with him, my daughter, in the paying of this debt, although neither of you will ever be able to repay a small part of what you would both like.

TAHA HUSSEIN

Notes

[1] Shaikh or sheikh. Means literally 'an elderly man'. Hence it is used among Bedouin for the chief of a tribe and among civilised Arabs for the head of an order or sect, like the dervishes. Shaikh has many other uses besides. It may mean a learned doctor of religion (there are no priests in Islam) or a senator. Here it is merely used as a title of respect for the author's father, as being the head of the family or one who has memorised the Quran.

Cf. the English word 'elder' and its Greek equivalent 'presbuteros' from which the words presbyter and priest are derived.

[2] Abu-l-'Alā al-Ma'arry. A famous Arabic poet, philosopher and man of letters. He was born A.D. 973 and died A.D. 1057. He was a native of Northern Syria and like the author of this book lost his eyesight as a child.

[3] Ramadan is the Arabic month during which Muslims fast from dawn to sunset, but eat during the night.

[4] 'Antarah and Zahir Baibars. 'Antarah was a pre-Islamic Arab poet and hero of Romance, a kind of Bedouin Achilles in fact. Zahir Baibars was a one-eyed slave who became one of the most famous of the Bahri Mamluks, who governed Egypt during the Middle Ages. His charge at the battle of Mansura, in A.D. 1250, won the day and led to the defeat and capture of Louis IX and his army of French Crusaders. He became ruler of Egypt in A.D. 1260 and gained many victories over the Crusaders. He died in A.D. 1277.

[5] Sufism or Tasawwuf is a kind of Muslim mysticism. The word is probably derived from the Arabic word for wool (suf) on account

of the woollen dress worn by Eastern Ascetics. Cf. the Capuchins who derive their name from 'capuccio', a hood.

Faqirs and dervishes are Sufis. 'Faqir' means poor in Arabic, and 'darwish' the same in Persian, or one who goes from door to door, i.e. a mendicant.

Zikr or Dhikr, which means literally mentioning or remembering (God), is the name given to the religious exercises performed by Sufis.

[6] Al-Burda. Qasidat-ul-Burda (The Mantle ode) is a hymn in praise of the Prophet by Al-Busiri, a native of Abu Sir, Egypt.

[7] Al-Azhar is a mosque built by Gohar, the general of the first Fatimite Sultan of Egypt, Al Mu'izz, in the year A.D. 971. It was made into a university by his successor al-'Aziz, and has been the chief seat of learning in Islam ever since. Muslims come to Cairo from all over the world to receive religious instruction there.

[8] Maghraby (literally Western) means 'belonging to North Africa, Tripolitan, Tunisian, Algerian, etc., etc.' The name is given to the tarbush worn by sheikhs and some country people as distinct from the taller and stiffer Turkish fez worn by the majority of Egyptians, apart from the fellahin. Tarbush is the Egyptian word for fez.

[9] Ta Sin Mim are three letters of the Arabic alphabet, equivalent to T S M. Twenty-nine suras or chapters of the Quran begin with various letters of the alphabet and their interpretation is uncertain. They may be marks recorded by an amanuensis when the suras were collected.

[10] Fuqaha is the plural of faqih, properly one who is versed in Fiqh, the religious jurisprudence or dogmatic theology of Islam, but commonly used in Egypt for one who is versed in the study of the Quran. Hence the word is difficult, if not impossible to translate. 'Religious lawyer' is meaningless in English, and one can hardly call 'Our Master' a jurist.

The word 'ulama' or 'ulema' may be found in the English dictionary and is the plural of 'alim, a learned man. As mentioned above, there are no priests in Islam, and ulema and fuqaha are roughly equivalent to the scribes, doctors of law, etc., mentioned in the New Testament.

[11] Monitor, assistant master.

[12] The opening chapter or Surat-ul-Fatiha is the first chapter of the Quran. It is about the same length as the Christian Lord's Prayer, to which it to some extent corresponds.

[13] Hud was an Arabian prophet, sent to the tribe of Ad before the Prophet Muhammad.

[14] Nafisa means 'precious' in Arabic.

[15] 'Mujāwir' means neighbour literally and refers to the people who used to live in the vicinity of the Kaaba at Mecca, hence it is used for a student.

[16] Sayyidunal-Hussein and Sayyida Zainab. Sayyidunal-Hussein is the name of a mosque where the head of Hussein, grandson of the Prophet, is supposed to be buried. He was martyred at Kerbela, Iraq, 61 a.h. (A.D. 680).
Sayyida Zainab is the name of a mosque which contains the tomb of Zainab, daughter of the Imam Ali and granddaughter of the Prophet. Both names are also given to the respective quarters in which the mosques are situated.

[17] The Alfiyya is a versified Arabic grammar written by Ibn Malik of Jaen, who died in A.D. 1273.

[18] The Unity (Arabic Tawhid) is the fundamental doctrine of Islam that God is One, as opposed to the Christian doctrine of the Trinity. Jurisprudence is, of course, Fiqh (see note 10).

[19] Malik means king or possessor, and is used here as a pun on the author's name.

²⁰ 'Ulema, plural of 'Alim (learned) cf. faqih, fuqaha, note 10. Qadi is, of course, Arabic for judge.

²¹ Qafs and rays. Ray is the tenth letter of the Arabic alphabet and corresponds to R, pronounced as in Italian. Qaf is the twenty-first letter and, although often transliterated q or k, has no equivalent in European languages. However it is generally mispronounced by Arabic speaking people, except when reading the Quran. In Lower Egypt it becomes a glottal stop, and in Upper Egypt it is pronounced like a G.

²² The Hanafite sect. Muslims are divided into main divisions, Sunnis and Shiahs, and the majority, including the Egyptians, are Sunnis. Among the Sunnis there are four equally orthodox sects, the Hanafites, the Shafi'yites, the Malakites and the Hanbalites, called after the four Imams who founded them, Abu Hanifa, Al-Shafi'y, Malik and Ibn Hanbal.

Cf. the different schools of thought within the Church of England, Evangelical, Catholic and Modernist.

²³ Pilgrim, i.e. one who has made the pilgrimage to Mecca, a hajj or hajjy.

²⁴ In the spoken Arabic of Egypt the two words for 'stages' and 'oxen' make a pun.

²⁵ Ibn Farid. 'Umar Ibn-ul-Farid was the poet of Arab mysticism. His diwan (collection of poetry) includes a Hymn of Divine Love, called Nazm-ul-Suluk or Poem on Mystics' progress, also a metaphorical Hymn of Wine, called the Khamriyya.

²⁶ Al-Ghazzaly. Abu Hamid al-Ghazzaly, who was born in A.D 1058 and died in A.D. 1111, was the great dogmatic theologian of Islam.

²⁷ The conquests and raids, i.e. of the Prophet.

[28] Ibn Khaldun was born at Tunis in A.D. 1332 and died in Cairo in A.D. 1406. He has been called the greatest historical thinker of Islam. In his Muqaddima (Prolegomena), which is the first volume of his Book of Examples (Kitab-ul-'Ibar), there is a chapter on Sufism.

[29] Hassan of Basra. A famous divine and ascetic who died in A.D. 728.

[30] Ya Sin (YS). The thirty-sixth sura is so called because it begins thus. It may be an abbreviation of 'Ya Sayyid!' (O Lord!) or 'Ya Insan' (O! Man!). See note 9.

[31] The Qutb-al-Mutawally. A mysterious and very holy Sufi saint, said to reside behind Bab Zuweila, one of the old gates of Cairo.

[32] Sham al Nasim or Shem el Nessim means literally 'Smell of the Breeze'. It is a great Egyptian holiday and is not connected with either the Christian or Muslim religions, except that like our Easter Monday it follows the Coptic Easter. It is probably the Spring Festival of the Ancient Egyptians.

[33] Alif Lam Mim Sad (ALMS) perhaps means Ana Allah Rahman Samad (I am God, Merciful and Eternal). See note 30.

[34] Hafs. Of the seven readings or schools of pronunciation, Hafs is the commonest in Egypt and Warsh in North Africa.

[35] Warsh. See note 34.

[36] 'Id-ul-Adha (Feast of Sacrifice) is the great Muslim Festival. It occurs on the tenth of the month Dhul-Hijjah, and is part of the rites of pilgrimage. It is held to be instituted in commemoration of Abraham's willingness to sacrifice his son, but Muslims believe it was Ishmael (Isma'il) not Isaac. Most Egyptians kill a sheep just as we kill a turkey for Christmas.

[37] The Baccalaureat certificate is granted to those who graduate from secondary schools in Egypt.

[38] Ibn 'Abidin died 1252 a.h. (A.D. 1836). The reference is to his Radd al-Muhtar, a commentary on al-Hasqafi's ad-Durr al Mukhtar.

[39] Fahim ya 'ad'a (Do you understand, you fellow?). Jad'a (pronounced Gad'a) – fellow or chap. It is sometimes used in the sense of 'Bravo !' or 'Good man !'